—SUPERCARS—

SUPERCARS

THE MYTH AND THE MAGIC

DAVID VIVIAN

OSPREY

Published in 1988 by Osprey Publishing
Limited
59 Grosvenor Street, London W1X 9DA

Sole distributors for the USA

Osceola, Wisconsin 54020, USA

British Library Cataloguing in Publication Data
Vivian. David
Supercars: the myth and the magic
  1. Custom-built cars
  I. Title
  629.2'222
ISBN 0-85045-823-4

Editor Tony Thacker
Design Martin Richards

Filmset by Tameside Filmsetting Limited,
Ashton-under-Lyne, Lancashire
Printed in Italy

To James

Contents

Acknowledgements

Some of the sentiments, ideas, arguments and, yes, even words in this book have appeared in *Motor* and *Fast Lane* magazines over the years. They have never appeared together, though, or necessarily in this order. My thanks, therefore, are due to the people who have helped me towards a better understanding of the supercar and—the most friendly and understanding professionals I know—the photographers who took the pictures that saved a million words (at least).

So thank you *Car* magazine and Mel Nichols for sparking the interest and giving me my first job in journalism, thank you *Motor* for the opportunity to drive literally thousands of new cars, super or otherwise, and thank you to the following photographers for making this book look so good: Peter Burn and Maurice Rowe of *Motor*, Simon and Mike of Clickstop, Mike Valente and Alan Levy. Special thanks go to Simon Firullo for his evocative illustrations, and to Kevin Radley, *Motor*'s man in Japan, for writing down the key points of Japan's 'new technology' on the back of a cigarette packet.

Introduction

There is a certain kind of motoring writer, once rare, now common, who goes through life never questioning what he says but saying it anyway. That he feels singularly disinclined to do anything else mostly makes him a bad motoring writer, but perhaps the only truly reliable litmus test of important motoring trends. Uninhibited by conventional intellectual constraints, and often liberated from his higher senses by a nagging desire to have a good time, the 'primitive' hack can regress to a barely-conscious state, stripped of social influences and professional protocol, the better to conduct a cogent dialogue on cars he has driven.

Cornered, he will claim not to remember what he was driving last Thursday—or, worse, dismiss it as

BMW's 286 bhp M635 combined supercar ability with saloon car practicality. Courtesy *Motor*/Burn

'Japanese'—and then massage any inkling of interest with the compression ratio of the Ferrari he drove ten years ago. To the casual observer, it might well be that the compression ratio of a ten-year-old Ferrari is more fascinating than a contemporary Japanese family saloon in its entirety, but whenever I have suggested in reply that the future of the supercar probably lies with the Japanese, the 'primitive' hack has invariably wandered off to pour himself another drink.

The first time this happened I thought it was a fluke, but subsequent experimentation has shown that it works every time. So, there you are: a useful manoeuvre to hold in reserve at parties. But what if the unthinkable happens and he just stands there and says, 'Really'? You could always change the subject. Alternatively, you could change his outlook on the meaning of life, parties and everything. But how. . .?

The outrageous Lamborghini Countach is the stuff of myth and magic. The author likes it but reckons it's overrated. Others disagree. Courtesy *Fast Lane*/Clickstop

I've long thought that books about supercars that are true to the genre can't help but be half-baked homages to evocative names and as benignly uncritical as the glossy brochures from which they draw their inspiration. This book seeks to be nothing more than a collection of stretched, slightly singed-around-the-edges essays, and my sole purpose in writing it was to be critical—both of the genre and

notion of 'the supercar' force fed to the public via the black, metal Habitat coffee table.

Doubtless, there are writers better qualified than I to debunk the myths and muster the genuine magic embraced by the modern supercar, but since none, to the best of my knowledge, has fancied the job, you'll have to make do with me. But don't be too depressed—we're in this together. For one thing, I don't know Enzo Ferrari on first- or second-name terms—even distant members of his family have ignored me. For another, I have never met Ferruccio Lamborghini in a dimly-lit Modenese restaurant; clearly, I haven't lived. These men have never had the opportunity to tell me what makes their road cars so special, or so expensive. Over the past nine years, however, it has been my business to find out. To test, with all the insight personal experience and the appliance of science can summon, the world's fastest and most glamorous cars. To drive them harder than would ever be possible on public roads and publish the verdict, be it good, bad or indifferent. To make value judgements about qualities which, some contend, are beyond value.

At *Motor*, the magazine that has paid my wages for the best part of a decade, such judgements can be made with rare focus and clarity: driving 240 cars a year sluices out sentimentality and misplaced passion with the force of a high-pressure hose. Only the hard data tends to remain, but even that needs interpretation. Sometimes, it contains nuggets of gold, sometimes just the fool's substitute. The trick is to know the difference, and intuition is seldom enough. The resolving power of context is a more powerful and incisive tool.

Over the next nine chapters, it's the context of the ordinary car that's going to show the supercar in its true light. The supercar, as we know it, is dying out. As ever, the new order is the product of evolution itself.

David Vivian
Maidstone 1988

its active constituents. If the result proves half as much fun to read as it was to distil from the events and scribblings of my recent past, it will be easier to feel more tolerant towards the tidal wave of blank, unthinking adoration that washes over Ferrari, Lamborghini, Maserati, Porsche and the like every year. I'm not trying to set the record straight, but to hint at a possible alternative to the blandly romantic

Youth's innocence lost

'There were great cars, but few were the paragons I had believed.'

Up to the time I started to write for one, everything I knew about cars came from magazines. I'd driven a couple of cars by then, of course, and crashed one so badly that it took a year to repair. My father, who owned what I had managed to wreck, could see I was shaken by the discovery that even a car with decent suspension and fat tyres needed to slow down for tight curves. If he was angry, he didn't show it. But by some curious paradox that afflicts the truly smitten, even such a violent introduction to the harsh realities of life seemed vaguely unconvincing.

The real world still lay between the pages of glossy, colourful car magazines. There, where oversteer was as natural as breathing, my father's Opel Manta would have made the bend with road to

The Countach was one of the most arresting shapes ever to roll down a road. It played the 'ultimate supercar' role with flair

spare. And my passenger couldn't have failed to be deeply impressed with my fluid car control. Instead, he was frightened beyond the capacity for even a stifled yell as glass rained over our heads and a suddenly liberated coil spring rolled drunkenly down that treacherous hill.

I was still at school at the time, and the resilience of youth made sure that the setback was soon forgotten. It wasn't long before I was again immersed in the exploits of Doug Blain, the incomparably outspoken, hot-shoe editor of *Car* magazine with a personal hot line to the people who really mattered at Lamborghini, Ferrari, Maserati and De Tomaso. A tall Australian with a healthy contempt for pulled punches, Blain drove all the supercars as often as he could and frequently dined, on company expenses, at the most intimate restaurants in the old-town district of Modena. He had the best job in the world, and I wanted to do it, too.

Although it pains me to say it now, Blain was a hero. His opinions mattered; he'd forgotten more about supercars than Mike Mercury knew. What I hadn't tumbled to at the time was that his quest for the blunt truth was tempered by a brilliantly imaginative prose style laced with powerful seams of tension and drama. He was the first in a long line of Aussie supercar gurus at *Car* who spun an alluring web of mystique around the Italian 'exoticar' with a unique adjectival armoury. Even to contemplate driving a Lamborghini Countach, for instance, it was necessary to swallow a metaphorical 'brave pill', and you could only drive it well along a 'sinuous ribbon of tarmac, snaking sensually into the sun-baked hills'. The style was determinedly adventurist and tinged purple, but the cars were real—you accepted the one to read about the other.

The closest I came to meeting the man was at *Car*'s old West Smithfield offices in the heart of London's meat-trading community. I was there to deliver my first ever freelance article—a series of interviews with owners of the then new generation front-drive Volkswagens—and I stayed to observe a day in the life of the magazine, then edited by Mel Nichols. The personable Nichols, another graduate of *Wheels* magazine from Down Under, seemed to spend even more time behind the wheels of Ferraris and Lambos than Blain had and, had I not already been stricken by supercar fever, his enthusiasm would have been infectious. I remember him telling me about the buzz he experienced from blasting down a motorway slip road in a Berlinetta Boxer. That 5-litre flat-12, with its miraculous spread of torque and unrivalled smoothness, was the greatest engine he'd driven. I was goggle-eyed.

At about five in the afternoon, Blain walked through the door. I recognized him instantly. Without saying a word to anyone, he walked past the desk at which Nichols and I were sitting and into a small adjoining room, mostly bare but for a table, a chair and a typewriter. Without taking off his long black coat, he sat at the desk and typed for 15 minutes; mute, unsmiling, glass-eyed. When he'd

finished, he removed the sheet of paper from the typewriter, placed it in a wire-frame tray and, in gloomy silence, walked out of the room. Any thought of engaging my hero in a serious discussion on the merits of double-wishbone suspension or mid-engine chassis design was still-born. The man looked completely pissed-off and, who knows, probably he was.

Soon after that, he left motoring journalism for good, I think to become an antiques dealer in rural Wales. Later I learned things about Blain that could have explained his resigned, sullen demeanour. At the time, I simply couldn't understand it: he was a great writer who drove supercars for a living, so what was the problem? It took me years to square what I had witnessed that day with my conscience. I don't think it was Blain's love affair with the supercar that had turned sour, merely the kind of expression it could find in magazines. If this was true, it was a trap partly of his own making, as he was largely responsible for creating the technicolour world these mechanical marvels inhabited and the particular lexicon he, and writers who followed in his footsteps, used to describe them. It was believable escapism for the reader, but an increasing strain for the writer.

Just how much of a strain didn't fully sink in until I had been working on *Motor* magazine for about six years. By then I'd driven and, more importantly, tested most of the important 'senior league' exotics and written about them with what I hoped was the required sense of pace, colour and insight. After an adolescence spent soaking up the entire output of Blain and Nichols, it wasn't all that hard to fall into the appropriate style. But what, at first, seemed right and natural came to feel false and forced as the supercar miles built up. There were great cars, but few were the paragons I had believed. There was magic, but it was balanced by myth.

It all came to a head over a couple of days in the late spring of 1985 when I set out with photographer Peter Burn to drive what was then, and had been for some time, the ultimate supercar. I'd driven the

A coach-load of French schoolkids disembarks for customary Countach inspection. Courtesy *Motor*/**Burn**

Lamborghini Countach before, but this was the new Quattrovalvole with its two 24-valve cylinder heads and alleged 455 bhp. Our purpose was to discover its top speed. The car belonged to our recently-made friend Barry Robinson, whose two-valve-per-cylinder Countach we'd tested at the Millbrook proving ground some months earlier. Now the QV was fully run-in, and Barry was as anxious as us to put its fabled 180+ mph maximum to the test, especially as his previous car had managed no better than 156 mph around Millbrook's high-speed bowl.

Driving to Dover and a rendezvous with the red Lambo, we'd expected it to thunder past on the A2, a fast-lane speck in the mirror, growing amoeba-like to fill the rear screen before becoming a noisy red blur past our heads. The Countach had yet to arrive and already I was thinking in high-speed prose. Old conditioned emotions, briefly forgotten, were surging back, dragging a trawl net of tired clichés behind. As in times past, exhausted adjectives were regrouping to do battle in a saga of speed and that peculiarly celibate seduction only the Latin exoticar can weave. If I'd let them, the tidal-force images would have engulfed us, sweeping us away to a familiar never-never land where roads are ribbons, horizons are ever menacingly Spielbergesque, and crumbling village squares aren't merely square but enchantingly ethnic. But we'd been there too many times before. To go back in the Countach, however tempting, was not our intention.

Nor was there time. We were chasing that top speed at dawn, a cold, indisputable figure that would provide the answer to the lingering question posed in bars that accept American Express from Surrey to San Diego. A figure that would seal a raw seam of speculation in car-testing folklore left gaping for years: is any road car capable of more than 180 mph?

We missed the ferry. As it steamed majestically past the chalk cliffs, Calais-bound, Barry and Lamborghini importer David Jolliffe rumbled conspicuously into town. Late meeting, heavy traffic: the apologies rang true and underlined the fact that even in the ultimate supercar you can't beat an executive lunch. The next ferry would sail at 8.45 pm and this time we would be on it, stopping off in Calais overnight before heading across the Belgian border at dawn. Our destination was the infamous Jabbeke section of the E5, scene of numerous high-speed record attempts in the past, perhaps the most publicized being that of 'JET 1', the Rover P4-bodied turbine car. We were all aware of the risk involved in attempting to run at more than double the legal speed limit. We also knew that the risk had little to do with the Lamborghini's ability to perform the task, or our virtually traffic-free timing for the run.

In the boarding queue for the Sealink ferry, the Countach collected more fingerprints than a murder investigation. Within seconds of its arrival, a coachload of French youths, olive-skinned and loose-limbed, had casually swarmed over every curve, scoop and bulge like an army of soldier ants

on acid languidly inspecting an alien lifeform that had strayed too close to the nest prior to dismantling it. One suspects that, probably having nothing better to do, they would have afforded the same measure of attention to anything moderately interesting. But the Countach held them transfixed, each one working through a private fantasy of what it would be like to drive, or even sit in, a supersonic sculpture. Coming from the land of two-cylinder, tin-foil, bug-eyed, four-wheeled mopeds, you could hardly blame them. And they were only the first group.

Everywhere the Countach stopped crowds gathered. It proved something: it showed that even people who own 2CVs or Ford Fiestas or Fiat Pandas are not indifferent to the notion of an innately superior motor car with all its elitist connotations. At least not one as forcefully expressed as the Lamborghini. I would like to think that most treated contact with the Countach as a fortunate diversion, but I can't help thinking that some went home dissatisfied with their lot and bought a stick-on plastic boot spoiler for their econobox the very next day. If so, they were cruelly deluded: we had to take the Lamborghini's off before commencing the high-speed runs.

At 5 am next morning, illuminated by the soft street lighting outside our Calais hotel, the Lambo's cabin looked invitingly warm and cosy. As we cruised through the sleepy Belgian border, the car's controls were good, sharp-witted company. At this stage, I let the V12's torque do the work. Driving was simply a matter of easing the car through the gears — a still deliberate task since the gearbox was tight with newness — and adjusting the throttle in fifth. Whatever we were about to discover on the Jabbeke straight, this much was clear: the 48-valve engine was both quieter than its predecessor (still loud by most standards) and tangibly more flexible. It promised a great deal.

We pulled into a parking area just as the cold morning light was peaking dimly over the horizon. There was rain in the air, but so far sensed only as a

Four camshafts, 48 valves and several miles of intestinal chains. Countach V12 wins the under-bonnet beauty contest hands down. Courtesy *Motor*/**Burn**

filmy dampness. More encouragingly, the long, straight strip of autoroute we were planning to use was all but deserted. Transcontinental juggernauts rumbled past with increasing frequency, but the gaps between them were still wide enough if we hurried.

Removing the winged bootlid robbed us of three minutes, fitting the standard item another five. It was remarkable how different the car looked— better, I thought, though Barry was undecided. What difference, if any, its absence would make to the Lambo's passage through the air we were about to find out as Barry notched the seat back and fired up. Unlike his old 5-litre car, the QV didn't 'explode' into life. The response to the key was instant, but the thunder more distant.

Barry, who naturally knew the car better than anyone, knew best of all how to deal with the sticky throttle that had dogged most of my attempts at

smoothness on the run from France to Belgium. He made no effort to trickle unobtrusively away from a standstill, instead blipping the accelerator past the point of resistance while swiftly, but smoothly, letting out the meaty clutch. The Countach surged forward with a single, growling reflex.

A glance in the mirror and we were on to the famous straight, accelerating hard. It didn't require the digital testimony of a fifth wheel to know that this Countach covered ground like no Countach before it. Almost before I had time to register Barry's progress through the gears, third was all through at just on 120 mph. The road ahead remained flat and clear, and still there were two more gears to go. Thus far, the speeds had been gearing certainties but, once flat-out in fifth, only our Heuer micro-split electronic stopwatch could be relied on to tell the truth, since rev-counters are no more dependable than speedos for absolute accuracy.

Now the kilometre posts were flashing past at less than 14-second intervals; we'd cracked 160 mph, but the push in the back had faded badly. The times were still edging down, but much more slowly. Worse, we were running out of road. Barry had spotted a pocket of slow-motion traffic way in the distance. Just easing off the throttle shed 20 mph almost straight away—confirming our worst fears about the high drag of the Countach shape, even without the wing—and the brakes knocked off another 70 mph in short order.

Our best average for the flying kilometre? A shade over 165 mph. I took the wheel in search of clear air, but we had become just another chunk of moving metal in the morning traffic. Hunched over a table of coffee and digestives, Robinson and Jolliffe could hardly contain their disappointment, and neither could I. It was a far cry from the textbook script we'd worked out the previous evening. There had been a little more to come, but how much? As the rush-hour traffic streamed by outside, we were convinced that our chance to find out, at best only fleeting, had gone.

We were wrong. The early afternoon saw us back on the E5, but this time south of Brussels heading towards Liège. Barry was at the wheel, looking for that elusive gap in the traffic. Then, over the brow, there it was: a clear road stretching into the far distance. The V12's bark hardened and, as before, all conversation ceased, the hollow wail of the engine note battling against the shrieking transmission. The aggression and energy of it all was breathtaking, and the ride uncannily flat. But as I looked up from my notepad, I realized how hard Barry was having to work to keep the Countach travelling straight. The Lambo was weaving gently, using up all of its allotted lane and more; Barry's hands were constantly making small corrections at the helm.

This time it was better, the run peaking at nearly 170 mph with a best average of 167.9 mph for the kilometre. If there was more to come, it wasn't much and, by the time Barry had to lift off, the oil temperature gauge was already advising strongly against further punishment. Removing the two door mirrors and single parallelogram-style windscreen wiper might have gained us an extra few mph, but the exercise would have been absurd and unfair. We had given the Countach a fair crack of the whip in realistic conditions. Like us, Barry knew that the only way his car would be capable of 183 mph was if it was hit up the chuff by a Porsche 956. He knew it probably wasn't the fastest production car on Earth. He liked the Countach for other reasons, but there was no disguising the pain that the truth had inflicted. He'd bought the Countach as an 'ultimate', and in one important respect it had failed his expectations.

My expectations weren't so high, but it had been a learning experience nonetheless. At least one myth had been laid to rest.

It's fast (167 mph), but not *that* fast. Countach QV. Courtesy *Motor*/Burn

Lamborghini Countach

The Countach is a bone of contention between motoring writers. There are those, probably the majority, who firmly believe that it is the undisputed heavyweight champ, the greatest exotic there has ever been. These even include journalists who have driven it. There isn't a schoolboy who would disagree, and *their* allegiances have mostly been formed by reading the words of those who have never had the dubious pleasure of squeezing themselves behind the wheel. That the Countach is a phenomenon isn't in dispute. As penned by Bertone

back in the early 1970s, *sans* most of the current version's scoops and ducts, it was one of the most striking shapes ever to take to the road. Even today it is uniquely outlandish and can pull the attention of onlookers like nothing else.

In that sense, at least, it remains the champ. As a driving machine I think it is overrated and always has been—a car obsessively concerned with the image of supercardom, but never seriously committed to realizing its true potential. This, in turn, has stood in the way of it giving full value, though it

hasn't stopped Lamborghini investing in a second-generation version with the sort of weight and drag figures the car should have had the benefit of for at least five years. That one might just do the 190 mph the factory have steadfastly claimed for the Countach in all its forms, from the original 4-litre car to the latest 5.2-litre Quattrovalvole. The QV's magnificent V12 probably has a real 435 bhp, but it needs all of that to push its impossibly wide wedge of

a body through the air at 175 mph: acceleration is nevertheless spectacular.

Arguable as the Lamborghini's reputation is, we shouldn't underestimate its significance or influence. In the era of the Porsche 959 and Ferrari F40, it is no longer the fastest or most exotic of its breed. But it still represents an absolute of a kind. It's flying on the ground, a comic-book fantasy in the metal. Its place in history is assured.

Lamborghini Countach (QV)

Layout: V12, mid-mounted, rear drive
Top speed: 173 mph
0–60 mph: 4.7 sec
Economy: 11–14 mpg
Visual presence: 10
Aural presence: 8
Dynamic rating: 9
Charisma rating: 8
Sum-up: Hugely overrated, though its acceleration is as stunning as its appearance and its intentions, at any rate, are pure.

Car and supercar

'It's like a nightmare tailor-made for Ferrari drivers.'

Barry Robinson's other car, back in 1985, was a Fiat Uno 45. In fact, he kept a small fleet of them as runabouts for his business. Although not one to hide the Countach away when it looked like raining, he drove the Uno about three times as much as the Lambo and confessed to enjoying it. Not in the same way as the Countach, of course, but it was nimble and fun and practical.

I'd only add that you can see out of an Uno's side and rear windows, it has a lighter gear-change, clearer instrumentation and slicker switchgear. It's roomier and superficially more comfortable, though, perhaps surprisingly, the Countach has the more pliant ride, even around town. Also, the Fiat is small:

Innocent Uno? Wrong. The Mike Spence Uno Turbo takes no prisoners. Courtesy *Motor*/**Rowe**

it takes up less road space, it can slip through slim gaps, it's more handy, more wieldy. It's a fairly ridiculous comparison, I know, and one that could easily be made between any serious 'exotic', where practicality is mercilessly sacrificed on the altar of dynamic gratification, and your cheap, run-of-the-mill supermini, where design parameters have to be carefully balanced. One is the product of inspiration, the other of compromise.

But wait. Let's assume that the Uno is not the anodyne 45, but the vastly more invigorating and interesting Turbo. At this point we must acknowledge the influence of the turbocharger over the past decade or so. But for the exhaust-driven blower, there wouldn't be a book to write: its impact on the fast-car scene has been as radical as the first pacemaker's was to cardiac medicine. Despised as it is by some for blunting throttle response and introducing lag, it has nevertheless redefined the

ground rules for those who peddle performance to the public.

Probably the world's fastest and certainly most 'exotic' production road car, Ferrari's 201 mph F40, is turbocharged and that, essentially, comes from the same company as the Uno Turbo. Ferrari's Formula One racing cars have been turbocharged, too, and you might remember that the original advertising campaign for the Uno Turbo milked the link with an epic degree of unsubtlety.

Even in standard form, the Uno Turbo is a remarkable and significant small car. Its X1/9-based, single-overhead-cam, four-cylinder engine delivers 105 bhp from just 1299 cc which is, as near as damn it, 81 bhp/litre. That's quite good but, even without artificial assistance, the 5.2-litre Lamborghini V12's 87 bhp/litre is marginally better. Since both Fiat and Lamborghini are Italian, it's probably safe to assume that if they are fibbing about power outputs, it's by a similar amount.

When it comes to applied technology, though, no one can bend the truth, and the truth is that the Fiat can't lose. Its major ancillaries are state-of-the-art and comprise Bosch LE Jetronic fuel injection, a watercooled IHI turbocharger, air-to-air intercooling and knock-sensing Marelli Microplex electronic ignition.

Now the real beauty of having a turbo supported by a truly integrated suite of electronic management measures is that, within reason, you can turn up the wick without serious fear of blowing-up the engine. Once such turbo temptations were fraught with risk, now the wonders of the microchip allow you to simply reprogram the management. Introduce water injection to keep combustion-chamber temperatures down when the boost is up, and suddenly you're looking at 131 bhp and a walloping 145 lb ft of torque: the magic 100 bhp/litre barrier—not so very

The Mike Spence Uno Turbo looked ridiculous, but could shut down a Testarossa between 50 and 70 mph. Courtesy *Fast Lane/***Cazals**

long ago the efficiency benchmark for a race-tuned engine—has been breached and the Lambo's legendary engine efficiency is lunched. Mike Spence Motorsport are responsible for tapping the Uno Turbo's unseen potential and will even replace the 'Turbo' badges with those from a 55 S.

The point is that, with a little help from its friends, the humble Uno has yanked itself on to a higher plane with relatively little effort. And remember that the Uno is a car originally designed as a shopping basket on wheels, a humble hatch untroubled by visions of greatness and harbouring ambitions no more adventurous than to deliver the groceries safely home after a mission to the local supermarket. Style doesn't come into it. It's an innocuous small box, with all the practical advantages that confers and one or two, usually ignored, that are positively conducive to fast driving.

More than being able to nip and tuck through heavy traffic and park in small gaps, a compact car can place its driver nearer to the crown of the road for optimum field of view around blind left-handers without hanging a bulging flank on the wrong side of the road. Thus it is that a mildly massaged Uno Turbo can move its driver and passengers, and all their luggage, about the countryside with the sort of haste that used to be the exclusive preserve of a Ferrari or a Lamborghini or a Porsche. There have always been tuned small cars, but none quite like this.

All right, a top speed of 124.1 mph isn't especially thrilling by supercar standards—not bad for a 1300, though—and 0–60 mph in 7.4 seconds is unlikely to see a Countach driver nervously slicking back his hair at the traffic lights. (On the contrary, when an Uno pulls up alongside, he's not going to make any conspicuous effort to out-drag so contemptible a machine, so the canny Spence Uno driver gets away first every time.) But top speed and 0–60 are essentially pub-talk fodder. Such statistics are vital for comparing the absolute performance of one car with another, but indicative of virtually nothing on

today's often crowded roads. What's crucial is the ability to overtake, the ability to accelerate between 30 and 70 mph without wasting time changing down a gear or two.

Here, the Spence Uno is intensely thought-provoking. Let's compare it with Ferrari's excellent Testarossa, a supercar powered by a 5-litre, 48-valve, flat-12 engine, held in even greater awe than the Lamborghini's 5.2-litre V12 for its sledgehammer mid-range punch. In fourth, this multi-valved marvel can accelerate the Ferrari from 40 to 60 mph in the twinkling of a Cartier watchstrap—a mere 4.4 seconds. To put that into perspective, and understand why the Testarossa is in the big league and costs as much as a house, we need a sensible benchmark and a pertinent question. How long does it take Porsche's 155 mph 944 Turbo to dispose of the same increment? The 944 Turbo, incidentally, is one of my favourite cars but, for the purposes of this comparison, it's going to have to eat dirt. That's because it's fourth-gear 40–60 mph time of 6.2 seconds, while excellent by most standards, is simply crushed by the Testarossa's.

So what of the Fiat? What can a 1299 cc tin tub with four cylinders and a turbo do against the Maranello mauler? How about 40–60 mph in 4.1 seconds? That shaves a cool 0.3 seconds off the Ferrari's time. Obviously a fluke. Let's try 50–70 mph: 4.5 seconds for the Testarossa, 4.4 seconds for the 1300 Fiat. It's like a nightmare tailor-made for Ferrari drivers. And it gets worse when the comparisons are struck in fifth. The Ferrari is good for a sizzling 6.8 seconds between 40 and 60 mph, but the Uno is an entire second quicker; from 50 to 70 mph it's an even more embarrassing story—7.3 seconds Testarossa, 5.2 seconds Spence Uno. As you can see, the little Fiat is just hitting its stride at this point. In fact, at all speeds up to the UK limit, the Uno has the measure of the Ferrari. It worries me that I possess this information. As my colleague John

Big, beautiful and red. The charismatic Ferrari Testarossa. Courtesy *Fast Lane*

**Founder member of the 'Brat Pack', VW's
Golf GTi still gets it right. Courtesy** *Fast Lane*

Simister wrote in *Motor's* original road test, 'there's
practically nothing this car can't overtake'.

Accelerating Spence Uno style is pure, no pussy,
supercar. It may lack the noise and the sense of
drama, but the action is the same. But don't presume
that it makes this astonishing buzz box a pukka
supercar in the conventional sense. It doesn't. What
the faceless Fiat does is rather more intriguing than
such a rigid classification could ever imply. It takes
as its own the logical *raison d'être* of the supercar—
specifically the ability to cover ground more rapidly,
safely and rewardingly than an ordinary car—
but without the traditional supercar hang-ups of
excessive width, minimal visibility, cramped cabin
space, heavy controls and even heavier fuel
consumption, euphemistically toted as the automotive equivalent of erogenous zones by exoticar
zealots. For erogenous read general convenience,
versatility and operational refinement.

Golf GTi 16V; ability beyond its price and modest origins. Courtesy *Motor*/Burn

The fact is that the Fiat has neither the brakes nor the grip of a contemporary Ferrari. (Yet both shortfalls are largely offset by its compact size and agility; wide cars need a lot of grip because they have less road to use if they start to slide.) Nor does it possess any of the macho symbolism central to the concept of a supercar. At the time of writing, Mike Spence Motorsport sold an Arnie Schwarzenegger body kit—all bulging arches and Testarossa-style slats—but, far from evoking the intended degree of sexiness, the result resembled an experiment in genetic engineering that had gone horribly wrong. A gerbil kitted out for the Super Bowl would have looked more sensible. The body kit missed the mark and the point.

We began this chapter with Barry Robinson's Fiat Uno 45 and, in two easy stages, the Uno has painlessly acquired a set of strengths and vital statistics that question the very validity of even a good exotic like the Testarossa. In most respects, the divisions between the two cars cannot be bridged, but what's important is the common purpose they share and achieve. That purpose is to put an extraordinary ability into the hands of the driver, to let him touch a raw seam of pleasure, to tap the magic of speed. The Spence Uno merely illustrates the point that such rewards are becoming more accessible and more affordable, as the sort of technology big car makers can literally buy in inevitably raises base standards.

As time marches on, the old-guard supercars stand still and the hi-tech ones advance the state of the art rather slowly, and very expensively. It's been a long time since a supercar needed a 12-cylinder, mid-mounted engine and double-wishbone suspension for basic credibility. Road-going adaptions of racing cars remain a purist form, but the alternatives are growing ever more persuasive. It's a measure of how rapidly the scene is changing, and the gap narrowing, that I can advance this proposition without feeling even mildly heretical. Even now, the stature of the orthodox supercar is being steadily undermined by the automotive equivalent of

Below **Grown-up Fiat X1/9, or baby Ferrari? The Toyota MR2 was a bit of both. Courtesy** *Motor*/**Burn**

Right **The toughest member of the 'Brat Pack'—Peugeot's 205 GTi 1.9. Courtesy** *Motor*/**Rowe**

Hollywood's 'Brat Pack', of which the Spence Uno is merely an extra-talented member.

The Brat Pack is growing all the time. Membership qualifications embrace a precocious talent born out of apparently modest and essentially unglamorous attributes and the ability to 'steal scenes' from established superstar performers. Founder members include the VW Golf GTi, the Talbot Sunbeam Lotus, the Peugeot 205 GTi, the Renault 5 GT Turbo and the Toyota MR2, though cars which have deliberately assumed the 'supercar look', like the Renault GTA Turbo and Ford Sierra RS Cosworth, aren't excluded.

My first real taste of what a Brat could do came not at the wheel of one, but during a long drive up through Scotland, with photographer Peter Burn, in a Jaguar XJ12—not a Ferrari, perhaps, but 300 bhp of silken muscle and a chassis renowned for its balance, poise and grip made a formidable combination. Back in 1986, there was no finer or faster saloon made.

No car I had ever encountered possessed a quieter or smoother engine. After lunch in the Lake District, I roused the 12 cylinders back into life. It wasn't easy to judge the exact moment the flame caught. The rev-counter flicked off the bottom of the scale, I released the key . . . nothing. Just the muted hum of cooling fans and the delicate whirrings of servo motors as the automatic air conditioning sorted itself out. I eased the gear selector back through reverse and neutral and past the dog-leg detent into drive, depressed the smooth-acting, floor-hinged accelerator and the XJ12 glided forward with an effortlessness that made me chuckle. It was a real edge-of-reality experience, almost absurd in its contradictions: huge power and great tranquility sharing the same moment.

Back on the M6, the XJ12 settled to a serene 80 mph, Sierras and Scorpios blurring past as if their drivers' underpants were on fire. The temptation to reel them in and spit them out was great, but I let them go, secure in the knowledge that very little could live with the Jag. They weren't worth the effort.

Next morning, on the part of the A82 that runs from Fort William to the southern edge of Loch Ness, I drove the Jaguar as hard as I dare. The road was a real test for the big car, punctuated, as it was, with vicious undulations, disguised dips and tight turns. For much of the time, I manually pegged the automatic transmission in second gear, the ratio in which the engine's vast reserves could be unleashed in a tidal flood to shrink straights like a pair of brand-new jeans.

The car felt absurdly rapid between the corners, and yet it was being unsettled by the road's crests and dips, the magic-carpet ride quality that had so impressed on the motorway suddenly checking clumsily or, at worst, scraping the Jaguar's belly along the tarmac. Each time it happened we winced, but there was a briskly-driven Vauxhall Cavalier SRi up ahead that I felt honour-bound to catch. In due course, we did, and its driver courteously let us by. I pushed on with undiminished enthusiasm, but the Cavalier refused to reduce the size of its image in my rear-view mirror. If anything, it started to fill it with almost intimidating regularity. Whether the Cavalier driver thought I should reciprocate his earlier gesture I have no idea but, if he did, he was out of luck.

Just before Loch Ness loomed into sight, the road straightened out and opened up. I flattened the accelerator and the Jaguar surged forward as if Mercury himself had lent down out of the sky and given us a push Dinky-car style. This was, indeed, a moment to savour. The Brat, and not a particularly potent one at that, had wrought enough embarrassment by keeping up through the twists. Now it was his turn to feel humbled by the Jaguar's mighty acceleration. And, sure enough, when I glanced in the rear-view mirror he was gone. In fact, he was nowhere to be seen. 'Must have taken that road on the left, just before the straight,' said Peter. I said nothing.

Peace and tranquility—Loch Ness and Jaguar XJ12. Courtesy *Motor*/**Burn**

Ferrari Testarossa

Locked in an endless arm-wrestle with the Countach, the Testarossa offers a crucial contrast in style and impact. Whereas the Lamborghini relies on its acute angles and aggressive appendages for visual drama, the Ferrari accentuates its considerable width (some 3 in. greater than its rival's) with flared slats and a shallow rear aspect. The overall effect is more conventional, but carries the advantage of subtlety without loss of presence. Somehow, the Testarossa

manages to look flash and understated at the same time: it's not as relentless on the eyes as the Countach. Or the ears, come to that.

The pro-Countach camp are fond of pointing out the sheer sonic magnificence of the QV's 12 cylinders, 48 valves, four camshafts, three carburettors and several miles, I have no doubt, of intestinal chains. True, it sounds as impressive as a Formula One car—from the outside. Inside, at speed, all you can hear is an unpleasant and very loud heterodyning whine from the transmission. I've heard waste-disposal units that sounded better. Not only does the Testarossa's 5-litre flat-12—toting just as many valves and camshafts as the Lambo's—match the Lambo in deed, but it lets its driver enjoy a real supercar symphony, unsullied by mechanical harshness. The Testarossa sounds like two Porsche 911s in harness with a very strong sense of 'stereo'.

Yet it has to be said that the Testarossa is a softer-focused machine than its great rival—a superfast Grand Tourer rather than a raw, red-blooded racer. The Countach has the edge on outright acceleration, the Ferrari a higher top speed and superior cruising refinement. For pure driving excitement, the Lambo gets the nod, but the Ferrari's fabulous flat-12 is endlessly fulfilling.

Ferrari Testarossa

Layout: flat-12, mid-mounted, rear drive
Top speed: 181 mph
0–60 mph: 5.4 sec
Economy: 12–15 mpg
Visual presence: 10
Aural presence: 9
Dynamic rating: 8
Charisma rating: 9
Sum-up: Far better than the Berlinetta Boxers that preceded it, and most other full-blown exotics, come to that.

A tangible heartbeat

'The line which divides competence from charisma is everything.'

That the Jaguar's magnificent V12 engine was touched with genius was plain at the time and has become even more obvious since that memorable journey through Scotland. The major advance in mechanical engineering BMW promised with their 5-litre V12 failed to materialize when the engine made its debut in the superb 750iL. No one could dispute that the big BMW was one of the world's finest large saloons, or that it matched the Jaguar for muscle power and response. The more alluring engine, however, remained the British one. Its smoothness was more luxurious, its sheer sense of ease still unsurpassed. Although the BMW unit was superbly quiet and very smooth, it sounded a little frenetic when worked hard, yet without the

The Aston Zagato put many a Modenese marvel to shame with its honest performance and safe handling. Courtesy *Motor*/**Burn**

compensation of the crisp snarl so appealing in BMW's straight sixes. It sounded too ordinary, it lacked the V12 magic.

The line which divides competence from charisma may be very fine indeed, but it's everything to the supercar. Take the Aston Zagato. The car got under your skin, went straight for the pleasure points. It wasn't the feeling of intimacy you sensed with a car like the Ferrari 328, but something bigger, more expansive and, ultimately, more rewarding. It had a lot to do with the engine, which I now have no doubt must be ranked alongside the V12s of Ferrari, Lamborghini and Jaguar as an all-time great. It rumbled into life—after seemingly interminable churning if hot—and coughed and spat, eventually settling to a lazy, but slightly lumpy, tickover which gently rocked the car. Snick the stubby gear lever back into the dog-leg first, ease out the meaty clutch and the Zagato would trickle off into the traffic with

Above **Supercar performance, stately presence—the BMW 750iL. Courtesy** *Motor*/**Rowe**

the easy-mannered docility of a VW Polo. You could see the traffic, too. The wrap-around glazing meant excellent all-round vision and, although you were only too aware of the aesthetically disfiguring power hump on the bonnet, the scuttle was encouragingly low, making the nose that much easier to point.

Into second, then third at little more than cycling pace. The engine burbled more sonorously and the transmission started to whine, but the tractability was extraordinary. A gap up ahead. You didn't bother to change down—just flexed your right ankle. The engine hesitated momentarily then pulled. You instinctively leaned forward a little in the sparsely-padded, but well-shaped seat to gauge the force pushing you back. It was smooth and

strong. Double declutch down into second and listen to the evocative pops and bangs on the overrun. You could have done this all day and still derived pleasure from the experience.

Mechanical musicality the Zagato had in abundance. The first real overtaking opportunity of my first drive in the awesome Aston demonstrated the kick that went with it. This time there was no hesitation, no throat clearing. The big engine hauled savagely, growling to itself like a suddenly threatened wildcat. The lorry I was following disappeared backwards as if tethered to a double-strength bungee, the same fate befalling the procession of traffic in front of it. It was all over in

Right **The delectable Ferrari 246 GT Dino. Compact, nimble and efficient, it created a blueprint for 'pocket exotics' like the Toyota MR2. Courtesy** *Motor*/**Burn**

the space of 1500 revs, but the road ahead was clear and my foot stayed flat: 5000 . . . 5500 . . . 6000. There was no more chance of leaning forward in the seat than there had been at the start of the manoeuvre. The Zagato was an intoxicatingly fast car.

Ferrari's classic 246 GT Dino could hardly have provided a starker contrast, yet the baby Ferrari's sheer delicacy and coherence lifted it firmly into the 'special' category. Purity of form mirrored elegance of engineering.

Its proportioning was masterful. Some criticized a conjunction of conflicting curves, but the charge ignored emotional content. Constructed from tubular and sheet-metal steel clad with aluminium panels, the 246 GT Dino was arguably the prettiest Ferrari ever made, far sexier than contemporary exotics from Maserati and Lamborghini, and the conceptual antithesis of Porsche's rival 911. The inevitable wastage of space exacted by its mid-engined configuration was superbly disguised by the graceful sweep of the buttress ribs extending rearwards from the flanks of the cabin for the length of the rear deck. That the Dino was almost as long as a Ford Cortina was hard to believe: it tricked the eye into seeing a much smaller car. One thing was sure: there wasn't so much as a millimetre of constructional flab. Like a muscled torso, hardened by the discipline of a martial art, the Dino's shape had *definition*.

Yet, just as muscle weighs more than fat, the Dino was also a heavy car, tipping the scales at just over 23 cwt. If its performance was firmly second-division supercar, it was rapid enough for most. It could reach 60 mph from rest in 7.1 seconds, 100 mph in 17.6 seconds, and go on to pull peak revs in fifth (148 mph). By 200 bhp standards, that top speed would be a fine achievement today (Ford's 201 bhp Sierra Cosworth is no faster). But in the sprinting stakes, Ford's supercar for the common

The Lamborghini Jalpa—better to drive than the Countach. Courtesy *Fast Lane*/**Clickstop**

man hits the benchmarks more quickly, cracking 60 mph in six seconds dead, and 100 mph in 16. Nor would the Ferrari win any prizes for fuel efficiency: hard driving meant 16 mpg or less, and few owners ever saw the other side of 20 mpg. Ferrari's cheapest car was by no means cheap to run. Then again, to drive it was to experience expensive sensations.

There was little excitement in the first miles behind the wheel, just quiet appreciation of the Dino's easy progress through town. Its steering, although scalpel-sharp, seemed almost too light about the straight-ahead, as if attached to light, viscous resistance rather than the front wheels. But faster suburban curves soon revealed the beginnings of real feel, the sort of feel that would build confidence when pushing towards the limit on roads that were becoming wetter by the minute. The low-speed ride was firm, but without any hint of harshness, the suspension working with supple and quiet authority.

On that special day, the South Downs spread out before us like a green desert under an asphalt-grey canopy. Pin-point droplets of rain merged into filmy ripples on the windscreen, untouched by wiper blades already lifting in the airstream. We were travelling quickly, accelerating hard in third as the pencil-black line of tarmac swooped deep into the cleft of a valley and out of sight over a crest. As the engine climbed swiftly to 7500 revs, it etched its unmistakable mechanical chorus on my mind. The jet-like whistle of the gear train, the hard gutteral howl of the exhaust, the busy metallic backbeat of cam chains and valve clicks: just as the mossy-green dunes to the west seemed frozen in time, so the noise behind my head lingered for an eternity. Even in a straight line, the Dino was entrancing.

A dab on the brake pedal and the small Ferrari shed 15 mph with a tiny, almost imperceptible, shrug as its fat Goodyears rode over transient surface irregularities impossible to see from the cabin. It wasn't instability, just a friendly warning felt through the steering wheel. Over the crest and we were into the next straight, sprinting hard. The road was bumpier now, but the chassis' reactions remained just as lucid and subtle. Damping that initially seemed too soft soaked up even the most severe shocks with impunity. Small changes of direction were accomplished with no more than a flexing of the wrists. The faster we went, the more delicate and direct the Dino's responses became.

On tight, damp bends there was understeer, no question about it, but backing off the throttle pulled the nose gently and progressively back into line. The lesson was quickly learned. More remarkable was that the Dino remained just as forgiving when the tail was deliberately pushed out under power. In this respect, few mid-engined supercars have ever matched the Ferrari. I found a long, sweeping, uphill right-hander and tested the Dino time and time again. On each run, oversteer could be achieved early in the bend and held precisely on the throttle before the tail snapped neatly back into line. It was all so easy, so natural.

So this was the Dino. The car's cornering power would not seem exceptional today: not even by the standards of a grippy hot hatch like the Peugeot 205 GTi. The steering, the balance, the sheer coherence of the chassis—they were special.

Ferrari Daytona. Even when it's standing still, it's doing 120 mph. Courtesy *Motor*/**Rowe**

At least as interesting are the differences in character between the two 'ultimate supercar' contenders. Controversy attaches itself to the world's fastest and most expensive supercars like Joan Collins attaches herself to make-up, and cutting through to the truth can be a messy business. You can't help but shatter some cherished illusions on the way. The Countach, as you will have read in the first chapter, was no more capable of travelling at 190 mph than Steve Davis is of smiling when he loses a snooker match to Stephen Hendry. The Testarossa's high-speed handling is less stable than the Daytona's, a car 17 years its senior. And neither car would be able to keep up with a well-driven, third-generation Honda CRX down a twisting country road—they're simply too wide.

Exoticars have never been cost-effective, but then they're more than mere transport. The desirability quotient of these two, even in the era of the Porsche 959 and Ferrari F40, is sky-high—the Lamborghini for its crowd-stopping looks, heart-stopping cornering ability and searing acceleration to 150 mph, the Ferrari for the towering flexibility of its magnificent flat-12, the urbane good taste of its interior and its searing acceleration above 150 mph.

A miniature Porsche 928? No, a full-size Honda CRX. Courtesy *Motor*/**Rowe**

Above **Early Countach, unsullied by wing and ducts, much as Bertone intended. Courtesy** *Motor/***Burn**

Left **Countach cabin, poorly put together, but looks sexy— especially in black. Courtesy** *Fast Lane*

Aston Vantage—a supercar of the old school, and all the better for it. Courtesy *Fast Lane*/**Clickstop**

The Countach, for all its flaws, remains the *hard-man* of exotics: next to a slick-shod racer, nothing can muster so much apparent grip or use it with such hair-splitting precision. The thing has carbon-fibre sinews. You didn't really know what steering response was until you had driven one. The Testarossa feels almost soft by comparison: its responses aren't as sharply focused, its heart beats more slowly. But what a heart. The glory of this Ferrari is, perhaps, the finest engine ever to power a road car; a unit that uniquely combines the smoothness of a Jaguar V12 with the full spectrum flexibility of a thumping, race-tuned American V8— all wrapped up in the aural buzz of what sounds like a 911 Turbo in stereo. Moreover, it possesses the refinement, the cabin comfort and the practicality to make it an everyday proposition. For me, the Ferrari is easily the more fulfilling machine, even if the Countach provides more thrills-per-mile.

But given a straight choice, I'd choose the big, old, front-engined/rear-drive supercars every time. Perhaps that statement makes me a retarded romantic, incapable of mastering the delicate balance of throttle and steering needed to keep a Testarossa or Countach in check on the very limit of adhesion. Perhaps it just makes me smart. Such miracles I am more than happy to leave in the sensitive hands of professional racers. The great joy of the old supercars (like the Ferrari Daytona, Maserati Khamsin and Aston V8 Vantage) is their honest openness—their obvious power is all the better appreciated for being within readily defined limits. You call the tune, not the car.

Ferrari 246 GT Dino

That the Dino was blessed with greatness from the very start I have no doubt. Its delicately graceful lines were not only more arresting than most rivals', but genuinely sexy. Not until the 308 GTB did Maranello produce a better shape. The Dino was great to drive, too, with the emphasis firmly on handling and dynamic finesse, blood-and-thunder straight-line performance being quite beyond the little car. But because everything about its chassis was so right, it could do more with its 195 bhp than

most exotics developing twice the power. In that sense, it was way ahead of its time and set an important example for cars like the Fiat X1/9 and Toyota MR2.

Some contemporary Ferrari 'purists', however, fell over each other to dismiss the Dino as a fraud because it shared its engine with a Fiat of the same name. That engine possessed only six cylinders and, worst of all, anyone who could afford an up-market Merc or BMW could afford a Dino. At least they were right about that.

The Dino knew nothing of the accusations questioning its legitimacy as a rightful member of the Ferrari family and sought the same loving care and attention as its bigger brothers. From those who

understood its highly-strung temperament and fragile disposition, it received the right sort of kid-glove treatment. Those who saw the Dino as a reasonably cost-effective way to enhance their image, however, did so at the expense of the baby Ferrari's. The preening poseurs neglected their new toys, as they had their BMWs and Jaguars before, and a lot of Dinos rapidly became very tatty indeed. Market esteem nose-dived, and so did prices. In the early 1970s, rough examples could be purchased for as little as £2000. The truth was they needed another £10,000 to put them right. Thankfully, dedicated enthusiasts rescued many from a premature appointment with the scrap heap and the Dino slowly matured into the valuable classic it is today.

I'd place it in the First Eleven. It was the *optimum* supercar, the consummate synthesis of size, pace and dynamic coherence.

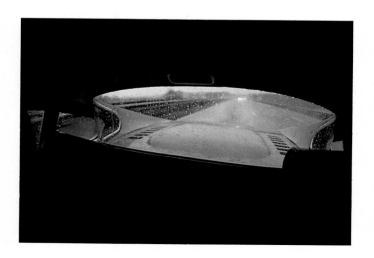

Ferrari 246 GT Dino

Layout: V6, mid-mounted, rear drive
Top speed: 147 mph
0–60 mph: 7.0 sec
Economy: 19 mpg
Visual presence: 8
Aural presence: 6
Dynamic rating: 8
Charisma rating: 8
Sum-up: The true jewel in Maranello's crown. Deliciously subtle charms, but fragile.

CHAPTER 4

Closing the gap

'The Integrale simply annihilated the sort of road that would test a skilled driver and a BMW M3.'

Performance, braking, handling and grip. Stripped to the bone, this is driving. Realistically, you'd expect the 'pure' supercars to supply the best thrills here, and they do. Whether they will continue to do so, however, is less certain. What's becoming increasingly and demonstrably clear is that the margin of the exoticar's superiority over the mass of amorphous metal most people drive is far less marked now than it was, say, five years ago. The ability gap is shrinking and will continue to shrink until that once vast chasm is just a hairline crack.

The inexorable march of evolution has a lot to do with it but, beyond that, volume car makers are setting their sights at what only a few years ago would have been thought of as stratospheric targets

Destined to become a classic, the Delta S4 was a devastating rally car. Not exactly slow on the road, either. Courtesy *Fast Lane*

for dynamic competence. Armed with the sort of potent technology only a fat research and development budget can buy, they're closing down the specialists' traditional advantage.

The results, at their best, are stunning and simply wouldn't have been credible a few years ago. Who could have predicted, for instance, that Ford would make a 150 mph Sierra with a peach of a chassis and the ability to out-accelerate a Porsche 944 Turbo? Or that the humble Lancia Delta would acquire four-wheel-drive, turbocharging and all-time-great status at an absurdly reasonable price? Fuelling the development of these giant-killers, of course, is the common desire of their makers to succeed in the arena of motorsport, not least for the publicity boost that winning can give to an entire model range.

Nor is it hard to determine which categories of competition have improved the breed. Rear-drive racers, like the Sierra Cosworth and BMW M3, owe

Right BMW M3 took to the circuit like a duck to water. Courtesy *Fast Lane*/Clickstop

Below Toyota Celica GT Four—great chassis but not fast enough to worry Delta Integrale or Sierra Cosworth. Courtesy *Motor*/Valente

Following pages Lancia Delta HF 4WD. Brilliant and a bargain. Courtesy *Fast Lane*

their great speed and fast reflexes to the track, while the more rounded, four-wheel-drive talents of the Audi Quattro, Toyota Celica GT-Four and Lancia Delta HF 4WD have been forged for rallying.

The Lancia's story illustrates perfectly the pace of development and how embracing the principle of 'the new supercar' steered its ailing maker out of the doldrums. Although the ill-starred Y10 supermini tried to sabotage the navigation system, the Fiat-owned car maker was blessed with a strong sense of direction.

Leading the way down Lancia's yellow brick road, the Ferrari-engined Thema 8-32 attained instant greatness in a sector of the market littered with talented performers. But if the 8-32 was the ultimate expression of Lancia's sharper image, the muscle behind the revival belonged to a more modest and all but forgotten model: the Delta. Star quality was a lot to expect from an unassuming five-door hatchback, modelled around Fiat Strada mechanicals, which spent the initial years of its production being just that.

The important date for the Delta, however, was April 1982 when Lancia displayed a prototype four-wheel-drive version. The Delta's destiny was signposted there and then. Four years later, the Delta HF 4WD went on sale. Making full use of advanced four-wheel-drive hardware, and powered by the injected and turbocharged 160 bhp 2-litre engine from the Thema Turbo, the 125 mph Delta 4WD looked far too good to be true. Almost unprecedented critical acclaim followed, most of it putting the Italian newcomer on a higher plane even than the Audi Quattro.

With the Delta 4WD already victorious in the 1987 Group A World Rally Championship well before the end of the season, and sales of the Delta running the Audi Quattro and BMW 325i very close in the European high-performance, four-wheel-drive market, Lancia launched the Integrale. This 'evolution' version of the HF 4WD was designed to keep the Delta on top, maximum power being raised from 165 to 185 bhp.

That power was distributed to all four wheels via a five-speed gearbox and epicyclic centre differential that nominally split the torque 56/44 per cent front/rear, though the values varied in line with the activities of the Ferguson viscous coupling, which limited the slip between front and rear axles by transferring the torque to the one with the most grip. The Torsen (torque-sensing) diff employed at the rear performed a similar function by ensuring that the wheel with less grip was not allowed to slip.

The Integrale was quantifiably a better car than the straight HF 4WD, Lancia avoiding Ford's example with the Cosworth RS500, the advantages of which could only be appreciated in the heat of competition. The Integrale built on the ability of the standard car with no apparent snags. Lancia claimed a top speed of 134 mph and 0–100 kph (62 mph) acceleration of 6.6 seconds. They weren't far off with the HF 4WD and, judging by the ease with which 225 kph (140 mph) came up on the flat, the claims felt about right for the Integrale.

More impressive than the cold figures, however, was the manner of their delivery. The ability of a good four-wheel-drive system to put the power down from a standstill is taken as read—the ability of the Integrale to stream past rows of traffic on a light throttle was less run of the mill. The beauty of its turbo engine was the way in which it combined blistering pick up with minimal lag. Boost pressure built up rapidly and early, which is as it should be, but too seldom is. Moreover, throttle response was clean and consistent throughout the rev range, and the engine completely untemperamental, despite the alluring twin-cam growl. The character of the performance was unchanged—there was just more of it.

The chassis could cope. Fluid in its responses, yet imperturbable in its control, the Integrale simply annihilated the sort of road that would test a skilled

An all-time great: Lancia's remarkable Delta HF 4WD Integrale. More user-friendly than your average Porsche 911

Left Overpriced and overrated, the road-going Ford RS 200 never really emerged from the shadows. Courtesy *Fast Lane*/Valente

Below The world's most practical and cost-effective supercar. Ford's original, be-winged Sierra RS Cosworth made you think twice about a 911. Courtesy *Fast Lane*/Clickstop

driver and a BMW M3 or the original, be-winged Sierra Cosworth. Its steering was astonishingly communicative, yet devoid of kickback or torque-steer, and provided a bend was entered at a sensible speed, virtually anything was possible beyond the apex. Set the nose in with a dab of brake, and the Delta would exit on full throttle with just a touch of opposite lock. Steer around normally, easing on the power progressively, and the balance was neutral. It wasn't the outright grip that was so staggering (it was good), but the sheer usable interaction of traction and power in a compact, nimble and civilized package.

The Integrale would have had more of a problem with the Sapphire-bodied four-door version of the Sierra RS Cosworth, launched by Ford in 1988. Any smug assumptions that the new, mature Cosworth was merely a sanitized, rebodied version of the outrageously-styled homologation special that changed the face of performance motoring two years before were dispelled by a virtuoso display of grip, suspension control and finely-honed cornering balance during my first encounter with the svelter Sierra on Sicily's roller-coaster roads.

In fact, that's not strictly true. My *first* encounter had been on the haul up from Catania airport to an old monastery-hotel nestling among the orange groves in Taormina. And that drive had been less conclusive. Local traffic was easy meat for the turbocharged, 16-valver's pulverizing pulses of mid-range torque, but there was too much of it stifling Sicily's rudimentary road system to be able to strike up a rapport with the car's chassis. If anything, the newcomer appeared to ride a little harder, yet change direction with less precision and verve than its fast-reflexed forebear. It was hard to hit a rhythm. The suspension changes devised by Ford's Special Vehicle Engineering operation dictated that I knew it would feel different but, at that stage, it didn't feel

A subtler Sierra Cosworth, the Sapphire-based four-door handled better than the original hatchback. Courtesy *Motor*/Rowe

fundamentally superior to what had gone before.

Chief among the criticisms of the original model's chassis were its edgy steering, a tendency for the front wheels to tramline and wriggle over transient camber changes, and a degree of pitching that could unsettle the otherwise pliant ride on punishing humps and dips. More worrying for some was the suddenness of the final transition from a neutral cornering attitude to oversteer. While there were reciprocal benefits to this hair-trigger set-up—most notably the super-sharp turn-in afforded by the lightning helm responses and the sheer adjustability of the cornering attitude in skilled hands—Rod Mansfield and his team of chassis wizards at SVE had considered the mix unsuitable for a car destined to be compared with paragons of poise like the Mercedes 190E 2.3-16 and the BMW M3.

I could certainly vouch for the validity of the comparison, having run a 2.3-16 myself for two years and had the extraordinary poise and precision of the M3 demonstrated to me at Mugello circuit in Italy by none other than BMW saloon race ace Deeter Quester. 'The feel is different,' said BMW's articulate racer. 'More safe.' *More safe* for Quester meant turning in early and pressing the lightweight trainer on his right foot so hard into the carpet it left the imprint of its sole there. What we were turning into was the Mugello racing circuit's famous long and demanding right-hander, a bend that in one neck-straining sweep takes you back in the direction from which you have just come.

What Quester was saying, in the politest possible way, was this: in a regular BMW 325i, we would have been pointing in the opposite direction long before the end of the bend—probably upside down as well. In the M3, however, not only was there every chance of completing the manoeuvre with the rear wheels following the front, but of completing it in some style and with respectable pace. For here was a 3-series BMW with a seriously well-balanced chassis.

Mansfield had explained that the improvement I could expect to find with the new Cosworth wasn't

merely a function of the Sapphire's four-door bodyshell providing a stiffer supporting structure for the Sierra's MacPherson strut/semi-trailing arm independent suspension, though it certainly helped. A lower front roll centre was chosen to introduce a little more initial understeer and take the sting out of the steering's response to small inputs, while stiffer spring rates (raised from 19 to 21 kg Nm at the front, and from 47 to 51 kg Nm at the rear) combined with softer dampers and a slightly thicker rear anti-roll bar to beef-up control.

Between Francavilla and Randazzo, and under the gaze of the moodily smouldering Etna, the road straightened out and the Cosworth hit its stride. Even from modest revs in fourth and fifth, it despatched the meandering strings of slothful, small-capacity Fiats and aptly-named 'Ape' three-wheel pick-ups with an expediency most of their drivers probably hadn't seen outside a gangland burn-up in Palermo. It didn't stop them driving belligerently in the middle of the road, though.

As with the original Sierra Cosworth, the revised version's mid-range wallop was delivered supercar style. Turbo boost could be tickled up by pumping the throttle but, mostly, it wasn't necessary. Lag, in any case, was minimal above about 2500 rpm, the accelerative surge solid and sustained all the way to the ignition cut-out at 7000 rpm. The Cosworth's 204 bhp was unchanged from the original model's, likewise the optimistic claimed top speed of 150 mph—145 mph would have been closer to the mark. But the 0–60 mph claim of 6.1 seconds erred on the side of caution. The test car supplied to us at *Motor* returned a staggering 5.9 seconds. The Cosworth packed performance-per-£ value not even the Integrale could match, and no Ferrari or Porsche could look at.

But perhaps I'm overlooking the most obvious link of all between the true exotic and the super-

Mercedes 190E 2.3–16 'Cosworth'—not as fast as its Ford namesake, but blessed with a superb chassis. Courtesy *Fast Lane*

saloon: the BMW M1. Father to not only the M3, but the M5 and M635 as well, the mid-engined M1 was conceived to meet and beat the might of Porsche in Group 4 sports-car racing, and the charismatic supercars from Lamborghini and Ferrari on the road. It never made it in Group 4 but, as a fast and beautifully-engineered alternative to the fragile Modenese exotics, the Giugiaro-styled, part Lamborghini-built, 24-valve missile was little short of a miracle. I well remember flying to Bavaria with photographer Burn to rediscover the M1 some four years after *Motor* had made the same trip to conduct the original road test. That day, Munich dripped under a soft-charcoal sky as we signed the M1's log, humped camera bags and tripod into the quite roomy (by supercar standards) boot behind the engine. After standing back for a few seconds to admire the still crisp and modern lines penned by Giugiaro in the late 1970s, we nosed the bright red M1 into Munich's early-morning mayhem.

First gear was long, the clutch on the snappy side of progressive, and the engine—that 24-valve masterpiece—racer-ragged below 2000 revs. We spluttered away from traffic lights, clutch-slipped out of junctions in a crescendo of wasted revs. Getting it right required a ballerina's touch on the loud pedal and iron control of the clutch.

The performance from the 3453 cc injected straight-six—277 bhp at 6500 rpm and 239 lb ft of torque at 5000 rpm—was real enough, but as treacherous as a cut-throat razor on streaming roads.

We pointed the M1 towards Austria and the mountains. The traffic was lighter now; the BMW was coming alive. Given the visibility to pass slower vehicles, the M1's tremendous 71 mph second gear came into its own, hurling us past dawdling pockets of traffic, seemingly mesmerized by their own sloth, with effortless energy. Extending the 24-valve powerhouse behind our heads brought aural rewards, too. At low revs and on a light throttle, the engine evoked something of a Porsche 911's metallic resonance—not quite as hollow, but just as musical. With the throttle wide open and the revs soaring

towards the 6700 rpm red line, however, the noise was quite different: a hard-edged howl of scalp-tingling drama and mechanical purity that massaged the senses with a savage vigour.

Yet this was just playing. Glimpses of the M1's straight-line ability were fleeting impressions. Too often we were engulfed in blinding spray. Filmy wet bends dictated cautious entry speeds lest the wide and lightly-laden front P7s ploughed straight on. Even at a 110 kph (68 mph) crawl, the M1's front tyres were skiing. The sleek Bee Emm wriggled and squirmed, its normally meaty and communicative steering suddenly as light as a pick-pocket's touch. White-knuckled, we pressed on at the same pace, spurred by the prospect of lunch in picturesque Seefeld, a few miles west of Innsbruck, and the urgent need to capture the M1 on celluloid. The message was clear enough. All the M1's towering performance and dynamic ability was useless in filthy weather: 1.3-litre Golfs and diesel 205s were quicker across the ground. It was a depressing fact, but one we would have to live with—until the skies cleared, at any rate.

The A12 autobahn took us past Innsbruck, joining the E17 towards Kitzbuhel. Action photography commenced on an all-but-deserted road winding up into the Kitzbuhel Alps, where snow was already settling on the lower slopes. We came across a sweeping hairpin bend above the lower cloud level and I was left alone in the M1 for the first time. It was a first-gear corner, but the M1's 50 mph ceiling in this gear gave me a broad band of performance to play with. Braking deep into the outside of the bend, I gently applied the power past the apex and the tail drifted progressively out of line. Half a turn of opposite lock held the slide steady for what seemed like an age before easing the throttle guided the tail straight again. Here was the magic we'd been looking for, the spark of ability that placed the M1's

chassis—already admired for its smooth ride—on the highest plane.

With night closing in and the M1 Munich bound, the weather suddenly lifted. Wet roads merged into damp roads, damp roads slowly revealed patches of dry tarmac. It was late in the day, but the M1 was about to be let off the leash. We rejoined the autobahn at Worgl, and the experience was memorable. The M1 swept on to the autobahn accelerating hard in second. I'd seen the gap 100 metres back and gone for it, confident that the charging Bee Emm could haul on enough speed to slip into the traffic flow without baulking a fast-closing pair of blazing headlights. Hard into third at 70 mph and the M1 was flying, the engine howling with delight and still delivering a mighty shove as it climbed towards peak power and beyond. We were still hugging the inside lane and the lights were still closing, but it was too late to back-off now. Into fourth at 120 mph and the lights were with us. For a fleeting moment the car pulled level. It was a 5-Series BMW, obviously a quick one, since we were now travelling at close on 130 mph. Then we were gone, the M1 sitting squat and stable into a long, long left-hander before disappearing into the night.

Around 400 M1s were made, many to meet a violent end on the world's Grand Prix circuits

Left **BMW's magnificent but ill-fated M1 had a lot going for it, not least its remarkable balance and poise**

Ford Sierra RS Cosworth

If you drive a car with both a powerful race-bred engine and styling that expresses 'speed' with an explicitness that is almost shocking, you probably drive an original Sierra Cosworth. And you can expect to be the centre of attention, so it's no good being a shrinking violet—the Cosworth isn't, nor does it make any bones about its terrific ability. Designed and evolved to succeed in the heat of competition, it passed on virtually all of the know-how and development expertise that went into its making to the road-going version and, at an original price of just under £16,000, was probably the performance bargain of the decade. A top speed of 145 mph and 0–60 mph acceleration of 6.0 seconds were impressive enough, but the handling, ride and braking, especially the braking, were so good that even the most cynical journalists went weak at the knees and slack jawed.

Its very existence is pivotal to the argument on which this book is founded. More than any other car, the Cosworth has been responsible for narrowing the gap between every supercar that came before it and the great unwashed mass of ordinary metal that plies the highways. It embodies both styles: the extrovert exotic with enough thrust and aerofoil area to lift a 747 off the ground, and the family rubbish bin capable of swallowing the kids, the dog, the grandmother and all that being a three-door hatchback entails. It's the car one man I met, who had owned four Ferrari Testarossas on the trot and crashed the last one, bought as a stop-gap runabout and kept.

Even as the plush and relatively understated Sapphire Cosworth, the fastest production Ford

since the GT40 is a hard-hitting road racer when the chips are down. In all important respects, it makes Porsche 911 ownership redundant. The only problem is the Ford badge on the key fob.

Ford Sierra RS Cosworth

Layout: four-cylinder, front-mounted, rear drive
Top speed: 145–150 mph (depending on model)
0–60 mph: 6.0 sec
Economy: 20 mpg
Visual presence: 8
Aural presence: 4
Dynamic rating: 8
Charisma rating: 7
Sum-up: Big-time supercar ability from a repmobile. Practical potency.

The new pretenders

*'A supercar must have a vein of raw excitement
that no amount of development can cover up.'*

One car capable of providing The Big Thrill was Ferrari's 160 mph 328 GTB, as lovely a car to look at as Ferrari had made in two decades when it superseded the 308 in 1985. Testing it for *Motor* was full of mixed emotions. Ferrari's entry-level exotic blasted around Millbrook's broad banking at an average of 158.5 mph, or faster than any production car we'd put around the bowl before it. On the other hand, it was numbingly noisy, sounded more like a tuned four-cylinder Fiat than a quad-cam V8 Ferrari, and was anything but forgiving on the limit. Beauty and the beast: the 328 was both but, by Maranello's own high standards, it lacked the charisma of a Dino or Daytona—or even a Testarossa.

**From modest origins, Porsche's 944 blossomed
into the company's most effective model.
Turbo (left) was superb, a realistic alternative
to the evergreen 911**

The distinction between soft-tops and sports cars, sports cars and GTs, GTs and supercars, supercars and sports cars, and so on is really at the hub of this book. What is clear to me is that most people's perception of a 'supercar' requires an exposed vein of raw excitement that no amount of technology can cover up. That's what separates Porsche's 911 from its 944 and 928 stablemates, and it has nothing to do with the fact that they also possess tremendous ability in all the conventional areas. Is the Thema 8–32 a Lancia or a Ferrari? Merely to think of it as a Lancia powered by a Ferrari engine is to take the car too literally, with scant appreciation of the inspiration behind it. It's like saying that sprinter Ben Johnson is a Canadian with two legs—factually correct, but lacking the proper emphasis. Ben Johnson needs the right psychological make-up to be the fastest man on earth, of course, but those legs perform the deed. Likewise, the 'Ferrari factor' must

assume a significance greater than its apparent contribution to the whole.

The principle was ably demonstrated when Porsche launched the 944 Turbo—a better car in most respects than the 911 Carrera, but no substitute in the eyes of most 911 die-hards. On a similar tack, the 911 Carrera SE aspired to be less exciting than the standard article by pairing its normally-aspirated 230 bhp flat-six with the bodyshell, suspension, wheels, tyres and brakes from the 300 bhp Turbo. The result might have been chassis overkill but, in reality, the changes did little to manipulate the indomitable square-jawed Carrera character. There was more grip and more retardation, both from the brakes and the broad-shouldered body (to the detriment of top speed in the latter's case). But the hair-trigger chassis balance and the finely communicative steering were the same.

At first, the Carrera SE seemed a rather pointless

Above **Beauty and the beast, Ferrari's GTB was both. This is a 308 QV, but later 328 packed a harder punch. Wonderful handling, until you breached the limit. Then it could bite back**

Above right **Four-door Ferrari or Ferrari-engined Lancia? The Thema 8–32 offered something of both. Engine sounded magnificent. Later versions had electronically-controlled damping**

Below right **The last of the Audi Quattros was the best. Torsen differential eased the edgy on-the-limit handling of earlier models. Quattro lit the way for the modern supercar**

car; pointless, that is, unless you wanted to indulge in the sort of serious posing only a Turbo could otherwise provide. In the end, I was forced to admit that it was a great 911—more finely honed, but still fascinatingly flawed and still a sports car, as well as a supercar.

We borrowed the 944 Turbo back to take on the redoubtable Audi Quattro—sadly no longer with us: the best front-engined car Porsche make versus a legend in its own short lifetime. The contest was intriguing, not least because the two cars were by no means the most obvious of rivals. The Porsche was more expensive for a start, and its 2.5-litre, four-cylinder turbo engine developed 15 per cent more power than the Audi's 200 bhp blown 'five'. The Quattro countered with full-time four-wheel drive, a superb rallying pedigree and an all-but-bulletproof reputation. The clash was remarkable for another reason, if you consider both cars' humble mechanical

Above **When the wind blows. Porsche's 911 Turbo Cabrio generates more than a light breeze at 160 mph—lifts the hairs right off your chest**

Right **A supercar engine has to look good as well as perform. The German penchant is for sculpture and order, as the Porsche 944 Turbo's underbonnet layout shows**

origins. The Audi's four-wheel-drive hardware began life underneath a military mud-plugger, while the 944 Turbo's design is rooted in the 924, a car that was destined to be an Audi coupé before Porsche took it on. Irony indeed.

And an epic struggle it turned out to be. The 944 had the Quattro beaten for pace, responsiveness, refinement and sheer flair, but the Audi emerged as the supreme ground covering machine. The more demanding the road and the worse the conditions, the more the Audi got stuck in, working unobtrusively with the driver to overcome all obstacles. The Porsche was beautifully balanced and could almost match the Quattro's dry-road grip, but when the going got tough, it took skilled hands and nerveless commitment to conduct the 944 at speeds the Quattro could breeze. Put the two on an autobahn and the 155 mph Porsche would be gone, chasing a lunch appointment in Austria with a fair chance of success. In the Audi—capable of 135 mph, but not much more—packed refreshment might be a good idea. At the end of the day, we called it an honourable draw, but were left in no doubt that we had driven two of the world's genuinely great cars.

In another significant junior-league supercar fixture, Renault's rear-engined GTA Turbo was thrown in at the deep end with Lotus' remarkable mid-engined Esprit Turbo and, against all odds, emerged victorious—albeit by the slenderest of margins and with a few provisos. Unsurprisingly, the striking Renault did little to alter my view that the Lotus possesses one of the most incisive and rewarding chassis in the business. Nor did its muscular and silky-smooth 2.5-litre V6 convince me that the art of turbocharging has advanced in the slightest since Lotus first engineered a blower on their 16-valve twin-cam four.

To drive along a sinuous road, I'd have chosen the Esprit every time, but to live with it had to be the

GTA. It was faster, quieter, more comfortable, easier to see out of and better finished. Given its unpromising rear-slung engine layout, it handled amazingly well, too—more predictably than any 911 in my experience. But for sheer seat-of-the-pants fun, a Caterham 1700 Super Sprint I drove soon after the GTA walked away with the laurels. The evolution of this jet-powered skateboard has been a lesson in economy of purpose, each new line drawn with the leanest of styles to preserve the minimalist philosophy from which the Seven was sired. The De Dion rear suspension meant that the rear wheels were less prone to jink over bumps, but it hadn't tamed the beast. That's still down to the driver, and may it always be so.

Toyota seemed incapable of putting a wheel wrong in the early 1980s. And if ever great things were expected of a car, they were expected of the new Supra. After the MR2, the Corolla GT and the Celica GT, Toyota were riding on a wave of almost unprecedented Good Press. Yet the computer-styled Supra turned out to be a product of very uneven ability. Few disputed that it looked the proverbial Million Dollars and, with no less than 200 bhp at its disposal, it should have been spectacularly rapid. But it was heavy and that blunted both performance and economy. Moreover, its twin-cam, 24-valve

Left **Perhaps the most audacious 'exotic' of all, the Lotus Esprit Turbo offered big-time supercar qualities at a bargain price**

Minimalist in concept and explicitly potent, the Caterham Super Seven sees off all rivals for thrills-per-hour.

straight-six was neither as smooth nor refined as it needed to be to gain credibility in its intended market slot. More bad news manifested itself as a tacky interior and a harsh ride.

When all seemed lost for the fat Supra, its handling saved the day. Few of us at *Motor* much liked its rather sterile steering, but there was no getting away from the tremendous bite afforded by its fat Goodyear Eagles, or the exemplary control of its suspension. The all-consuming American market was unlikely to disapprove.

In many ways, the first half of the decade belonged to the fast coupé at all levels, a market into which the Japanese finally, inevitably and irre-vocably sank their teeth. Mazda's restyled RX-7 needed to make no apologies for its Porsche-like shape: looks were matched by deeds. Even more impressive, however, was the Celica GT from

Toyota, which took on all-comers for the undisputed coupé crown and won fairly and squarely. Surprisingly for some, the strongest competition came from Ford's 2.8-litre Capri Injection, a car which had seemed to be on the brink of retirement for the previous five years. Yet, in a rugged, old-fashioned way, the Capri captured the essential spirit of the affordable coupé: instant visual appeal, strong performance and high entertainment value. It offered some soul to contrast with the Celica's cold efficiency.

More interesting still, however, had been the on-going battle of the 'hot hatches', a contest which literally redefined baseline standards for the whole of the motor industry. The big needle was between the French and German camps, reaching a memor-able peak when VW fielded the long-awaited 16-valve version of their Golf GTi and Peugeot sorted

Left 1988 Lotus Esprit Turbo was smoother than its predecessor, and faster

Above Daihatsu Charade GT ti, claimed to be the world's swiftest 1-litre production car

out the 1.9-litre versions of their 205 and 309 GTis. The 205 and Golf came out at around the same time, so comparisons were inevitable. What emerged was that the broad-shouldered little Pug—while hugely enjoyable and unsurpassed as a pure driving machine—was seriously outpointed in the areas of accommodation, comfort and build. It was a brilliant lightweight taking on a wily, accomplished middleweight. It stayed the distance and proved fast on its feet but, ultimately, had to give best to the Golf's more complete and polished skills.

Thus, the 309 GTi arrived with a score to settle on behalf of its little brother. At *Motor*, the arch opponents met the injected 2-litre version of Vauxhall's Astra GTE on the roads of North Wales in a three-way contest to fill the vacant 'hot hatch' title. Muscular and competent as the Vauxhall turned out to be, it was comfortably outclassed by its continental peers which, as predicted, were closely matched. But where the 205 had lost out to the Golf on space and comfort, the Golf now had to give ground to the 309. Moreover, the 309 displayed even more responsive handling than its smaller stablemate

Porsche's 928S—a fine car, but not the 'great' it once was. S2, pictured below, is preferable to S4, which had harsher chassis, massive price

and combined this with better balance and finesse, and a greater degree of fluidity, thus asserting a significant dynamic advantage over the VW. Despite the Golf's superior performance, build and finish, the overall verdict had to be tipped in favour of the superbly judged and coherently talented Peugeot.

A better soldier for VW turned out to be the 16-valve Jetta GT which, while unable to cover ground quite as swiftly as the racer-taut 309, provided even more pleasure in the attempt. The key to this appeared to be an engine with an almost limitless appetite for revs, a chassis with beautifully progressive responses, and major controls blessed with perfect weighting. The Jetta just flowed over the road, forgiving mistakes and flattering any brief flashes of talent.

But the real sensation of this class, the most audacious new pretender of all, was the turbocharged, twin-cam, 1-litre Daihatsu Charade GT ti. Here was an unlikely machine with the tools and the talent: great straight-line speed, bags of low-down pull for punching out of tight turns, unerringly crisp and consistent steering, and superb throttle adjustability. All this and a sound like an angry 911.

Meanwhile, Porsche's UK fortunes were looking anything but healthy as model prices continued to escalate and sales decline. *Motor*'s verdicts on the 928 S4 and the 944S, both of which appeared to us to be retrograde steps, rubbed salt into the wound. Personally, the 928 S4 was a crushing let-down, its admittedly tremendous potential compromised by a distinctly uncooperative automatic transmission and a board-hard ride. Try as I might, I couldn't get into synch with the car, and there speaks someone who had previously rated the 928 as one of the all-time greats. The problem with the 944S was that its 16-valve engine—while a reasonable example of its kind—entirely lacked the meaty, deep-chested flexibility of its eight-valve counterpart. The S was faster outright, but its performance was less friendly, less usable. A shame.

Returning to the 928 S4, for a moment, allows me a link to an altogether more impressive machine via a

tale recounted to me by a well-known car dealer with a show-business client (both of whom wish to remain anonymous). The car dealer delivered an S4 to the client's house for a test drive, but this didn't close the sale: he was singularly unimpressed. The car dealer's colleague, however, had driven down in another powerful V8-engined car of similar value. It was suggested that the client might like to give this one a whirl, but he declined on the grounds that it wasn't his sort of car. The car dealer pressed the point and offered to leave the car overnight. When he returned the next morning, a cheque for the required amount was waiting for him.

I'm not in the least bit surprised, for the car in question was the AMG 560E—aka Hammer—that we'd tested barely a week earlier. The test session itself had been a historic event because, at

The AMG 560E, aka Hammer, gave 'Q-car' a whole new meaning. Rapid enough to face down a Ferrari GTO, it could be driven by your granny

Millbrook, the Merc 300-based Hammer simply blew away all existing performance records for automatic saloons by lapping the high-speed bowl at 164 mph and accelerating from 0 to 60 mph in a staggering 5.0 seconds. Here was an unassuming automatic Mercedes with the performance of a Ferrari GTO (another independent test on a more suitable circuit credited the AMG with a top speed of 183 mph, some 4 mph better than a GTO managed on the same day) that your grandmother could drive to the post office to collect her pension.

The 911 is the most enduring and enigmatic of all supercars. It is impossible to define 'supercar' without thinking of the perpetual Porsche; the car, the strands of ability it weaves in the fabric of the breed, both black and white. I've talked to good drivers who would rather walk than drive a 911: the old-fashioned cabin annoys, the clonky gear-change irritates, the wayward on-the-limit handling caused by having the engine in the boot frightens. I know others who are loathe to drive anything else, relishing the very challenge it poses, slaves to the sounds and actions of that charismatic flat-six—and to its awesome performance if turbocharged— spoiled by the superb build quality a relative practicality. Porsche claim to have wanted to retire the 911 for some time and, but for the enthusiastic and undiminished demand, probably would have; and yet it forms the basis for what many believe to be the world's ultimate car—the four-wheel-drive, twin-turbo, £170,000 (£250,000, £500,000?) 959.

For my part, I'm a hopeless fan of the engine, though I'm sure I couldn't live with the rest of the car. It's not one that suffers bouts of laziness. Always

in the mood for serious motoring, there's little that could be mistaken for compromise in its character if you're not. The gear-change, for example, requires as much concentration to work smoothly in traffic as it does when you're blasting down a Welsh valley, low-flying Tornado filling the rear-view mirror. The

pedals unnaturally sprout up from the toeboard like disfigured mushrooms, the switchgear is exquisitely haphazard, and important sections of the instrumentation are obscured by the steering wheel.

The Porsche's big problem is that it never lets you forget about its shortcomings; you can only enjoy the *driving* once the machine has been mastered. By the standards of most modern fast cars, that's a perverse challenge.

Porsche 911 (Turbo)

Layout: flat-six, rear-mounted, rear drive
Top speed: 160 mph
0–60 mph: 5.3 sec
Economy: 16 mpg
Visual presence: 7
Aural presence: 7
Dynamic rating: 6
Charisma rating: 9
Sum-up: The original supercar cuts the mustard with turbo power, though Carrera drives better.

F is for fake

'Crockett and Tubbs were in a kit car with a powerful tape machine reciting Ferrari V12 noises under its long plastic bonnet.'

I switched on the television one night and, like every other night, designer America flooded into my living room. This time, we were pounding the streets of Miami in a fast car. Crockett looked as worried as a man earning hundreds of dollars a minute, driving a Ferrari Daytona and wearing a pair of Ray Ban Wayfarers can look. Tubbs looked as worried as a man who never looks less cool than his partner, but is invariably denied the opportunity to discern the extent of the concern showing in his partner's seriously-shaded eyes can look. The director of *Miami Vice*—the syndicated US macho version of *Frocks on The Box*—probably looked more worried than both of them, and with good reason. He had a potentially exciting car chase on his hands. This was

Lynx D-Type. Not as valuable as the original, but wonderfully evocative. Courtesy *Fast Lane*

an eventuality his agent hadn't anticipated when signing him up for a season with the stubble boys.

What the dandy designer detectives were chasing this time was a stereotype Greasy Spic Dago Wop pimp with a Spiteful Disposition, A Big Knife, Mafia Connections and a Lamborghini Countach LP 500 S Quattrovalvole which, at this moment, he was driving with typical Latin Flair, Crockett and Tubbs in pastel pursuit. The Jan Hammer soundtrack and Hugo Boss suits suddenly seemed less distracting—Daytona versus Countach filled the screen. This I wanted to see.

Greasy shifted down and the Lambo growled thunderously. Crockett shifted down and the Daytona Spider growled thunderously. The two great Italian exotics were locked in quad-cam combat, matched to within a sodium-filled valve of an inch as they weaved furiously through the strategically spaced Miami traffic. Which, of course, didn't make any sense at all for, as regular *Miami Vice* watchers will know, only the Lamborghini was real. Crockett and Tubbs were in a kit car with a powerful tape machine reciting Ferrari V12 noises under its long plastic bonnet. You couldn't blame them for looking worried. In the end, the Countach made a sharp left in a desperate bid to shake off the pacier editing lavished upon the Daytona which, by this time, had its tape player on 'fast-forward'. It worked. Indeed, it had to if the episode wasn't to finish 45 minutes early. Crockett and Tubbs had another four outfit changes to get through before finally nailing Greasy.

Of course, there are good reasons why the makers of even big-budget nonsense like *Miami Vice* should baulk at the idea of letting a rare and valuable supercar be driven by a man who spends a lot of time checking out his stubble in the mirror—both financial and, one would hope, moral. The joke implicit in all of this, however, is that in a show which draws its appeal from the dubious ethos of the Designer Label, the most conspicuous example should be a shameless fake. Equally instructive is that the fake is considered accurate enough to fool most of the viewers for most of the time. This is either cynical or pragmatic, depending on your point of view. It hardly warrants saying that it is the image and not the substance that is important when an overwhelming sense of *style* has invaded your psyche—provided it looks right, the compromises can be made elsewhere. If they can't be seen, who'll know the difference?

Well, *you* will. But what's okay for the *Vice* boys . . . I have a nagging feeling that the casually-flicked ash from one of Crockett's expensive untipped cigarettes has unwittingly ignited the blue touch paper to a substitute supercar business that was previously content to concern itself with AC Cobra and Ford GT40 copies. So rapidly is the new 'Italian exoticar' element expanding that plastic, Rover V8-engined Daytona lookalikes are already old hat. What everyone wants now, of course, is a plastic, Rover V8-engined Countach. And there are a

handful of companies prepared to sell you just that. One I visited was based in Poole, Dorset, and made a pseudo-Countach called the Primo.

After much polishing, the prototype Primo was ready to roll. Unfortunately, its gleaming appearance only served to highlight the appalling fit of the doors, one-piece engine canopy and boot. I suggested that, being a prototype, it should mirror Lamborghini's proto' Countach, which had dull, sun-faded paintwork, numerous dents and scratches, strips of black tape dangling from the bodywork where they had previously held test equipment cables secure and, most important of all, a few well-placed yellow wax-chalk marks to denote whatever it is well-placed yellow wax-chalk marks denote. Then the interior, which had no headlining, an instrument binnacle held in place by contact friction with the windscreen, pedals severely offset to the left and numerous exposed cables would have looked completely authentic and convincing instead of plain tatty. The psychology of the car was all wrong.

To drive, though, the Primo was all right. It wasn't much like the real thing, naturally enough—in some respects, it was better—but it did give an accurate representation of a very wide car with no rearward visibility, no headroom and an awkward gear-change. Although the latter had only the four speeds of the Renault 20 from which the gearbox was taken, the challenge was enhanced by the back-to-front gate where first was where second should have been, second was where first should have been, third was where fourth should have been, and so on. Contestants on *The Krypton Factor* have an easier time than this. The good news was a low-speed ride that was supple, yet taut, direct and accurate steering, and simply excellent handling. Structural integrity felt very good indeed, and the old Rover V8 certainly made a suitably menacing noise without

Just the thing for the streets of Miami—a replica Countach. Courtesy *Fast Lane*/**Levy**

being *too* loud—and that without any bulkhead sound deadening—though it didn't push the notoriously unaerodynamic Countach body along with much urgency.

But then that's hardly the point. The Primo was gawped at by the same people who would gawp at the real thing. So long as they didn't get too close, the fantasy remained intact. You can't argue against this; people who want a Countach, but don't have enough money to buy one are unlikely to beat a path to Lotus' door for an Esprit Turbo, even if they realize that it's the only sensible thing to do. Alternatively, you could carry the whole affair off with a great deal more style and panache. All you need is a Lynx D-Type.

It is doubtful if there are words to accurately describe the way a 4.2-litre Lynx D-Type sounded on the overrun. If they exist, I don't know what they are. A stricken Hawker Hurricane in a spiralling, tumbling dive to oblivion is one aural image that springs to mind. A sperm-whale dying of terminal flatulence is another, though such things strike me as being no easier to put into words than the exhaust note. So I won't try.

Of the sound's effect on those who heard it, however, I can tell you two things. First, it made you go ever so slightly deaf. Second, if you allowed the exhaust to let rip under a bridge or sandwiched between two brick walls, you could almost feel the pressure waves drum-rolling off your skull. A unique experience.

There were two ways of dealing with this. Either you stuffed cotton wool into your ears and looked embarrassed at being the focal point of so much unseemly noise, or you stuffed your head into an embarrassing hat—a leather flying cap and goggles are traditional—and revelled in time spent with Lynx's stunningly faithful replica of what many regard to be the greatest of all post-war sports cars: the D-Type Jaguar.

Can't afford a Countach? Esprit Turbo is the best choice. Courtesy *Fast Lane*/**Clickstop**

Trumpet chorus courtesy of Lynx D-Type. Courtesy *Fast Lane*

These were the choices. Like the real thing, the Lynx offered no compromises, none of the creature comforts even the driver of a Lotus Seven would take for granted. There was no heater and no roof. If it rained you got wet, if it was cold you froze. The blaring, gutteral exhaust noise was a constant, garrulous companion. If you ever felt like reaching for the 'volume' knob to turn it down, you knew the Lynx was not for you. It was driving undiluted. Every journey stung the senses like smelling salts, cut through mental fug with the measured menace of a machete, made your eyes water.

To own a Lynx with conviction was to believe that being cold was invigorating, wearing clothes heavy with rain water refreshing, and announcing your presence with a perfectly-tuned raspberry a social grace. According to the Lynx order book, at least three people every year become solemn adherents of this philosophy. Furthermore, they pay the best part

of £50,000 for the privilege and have to wait six months for delivery.

You've probably twigged. The Lynx D-Type wasn't very much of a hardship. What people queuing for a bus felt as you rumbled by, blue-nosed and grinning, wasn't sympathy but envy. What they couldn't see was just as evocative: a fighter-like cockpit—all bare aluminium and pop-rivets, precision toggle switches and exposed black relay boxes. You almost felt you should tap the glass-faced dials into flickering life, like a World War 2 Spitfire ace preparing to do battle. They were big and plainly marked, never more than the flick of an eye away from your low line of sight. You could see the important ones through the gentle arc of the large, laminated-wood-rim steering wheel which, like every other part of the D-Type, save for the engine, the transmission and the suspension, was made in-house by a highly-skilled and motivated workforce.

Each wheel took a week to make, which seems excessive only to someone who hasn't spent 150 hours fashioning the nose section from flat sheets of aluminium. D-Type customers didn't have a pressing date with the *24 Heures du Mans*, and Lynx didn't mind taking all the time they needed to get it right. The switches were sited on those parts of the black-crackle dash not occupied by dials or warning lights—a layout which eschewed ergonomics for a plainer logic. They wore no labels, as if to intimidate the first-timer, but worked with crisp precision. More significantly, they mirrored Jaguar's original design with an authenticity that somehow transcended the merely tangible. Like Rubenstein performing Beethoven, there is more to a polished recital than playing the notes in the right order. And the D-Type is a harder act to reproduce in spirit than it is in form.

The D-Type. What is there to say that hasn't already been said? It won Le Mans three times in a row, after nearly tasting victory first time out in 1954. It was, and is, one of the most dramatically beautiful sports cars ever made. And, of course, it spawned the E-Type, which distilled the essential elements of its design into the greatest road-going sports car of its day. In the Lynx, the E-Type repaid its debt to an illustrious forebear. An immensely strong aluminium monocoque centre section—virtually identical to that shared by D and E—carried E-Type subframes fore and aft, and on to this structure was bolted the E-Type's all-independent suspension, dohc straight-six XK engine (3.8 or 4.2 litres) and four-speed transmission, an alloy header tank, a special wide-base lower wishbone at the rear, a shortened propshaft and a foam-filled alloy petrol tank. The Lynx was considerably lighter than the E-Type, and the suspension modified accordingly. Lynx removed one of the pair of coil springs from each side, and fitted Koni dampers all round. The original D-Type, of course, used a live axle. Braking was also improved with discs supplanting the rear drums, a twin servo and a split circuit.

The crowning glory, however, was the hand-made alloy bodywork fashioned by Lynx, using traditional equipment which allowed them to undertake double-curvature sheet-metal work. This is famously time-consuming, but the Hastings-based company had recently doubled its working space to increase throughput, which reduced delivery for the D-Type from 18 to six months. Making the monocoques in batches and equipping each working bay with its own dedicated parts store further streamlined the operation. Even so, the time and effort expended on the manufacture of the monocoque and the body represented more than half the total cost of production.

In all, 63 D-Types were made by Jaguar, not all of which survive. Some that do live in California, where they swap hands for up to £900,000—or as much as an original Ferrari GTO. There are more valuable cars, but most of them are static exhibits in museums. Even ex-Weslake engineer Guy Black—a confessed D-Type fanatic—couldn't have foreseen the price explosion when he formed Lynx Cars in 1969. Back then, Lynx were the acknowledged experts in the restoration and refurbishment of Cs and Ds. It wasn't until 1973, when Guy went into partnership with Chris Keith-Lucas, that the company decided to actually revive the classic old-timer. In the ensuing decade about 30 have been made, both long and short nose and some from kits in the early days (no longer offered). Demand for the ready-built item, however, is stronger than ever, and with good reason. If you bought a Lynx D-Type for £15,000 in 1977, it would fetch about £48,000 today. Like the real thing, the Lynx more than holds its value.

57 SAL, a slightly wrinkled but utterly beautiful metallic turquoise long-nose, was bought by Lynx from a heartbroken owner who couldn't really afford it. We can sympathize. It used a 4.2-litre XK unit with an easy-breathing, big-valve head and an

Above **When a fake is as good as the Lynx, there's no need for excuses. Courtesy** *Fast Lane*

Right **Lynx cockpit details are authentic, the goggles a necessity. Courtesy** *Fast Lane*

alleged 300 bhp. Believe it, SAL was a brutally fast car. Prod the accelerator hard in first and the car displaced itself 50 yards in space. It thumped a hole in the air and filled it with the bark of its fast disappearing exhaust. With little more than a ton to propel through the air, it hit 60 mph in 5.3 seconds, and 100 mph in 13.1 seconds. The Porsche 911 Turbo driver who took on this Jaguar was sadly misguided. But for the meagre traction afforded by the large, yet slim, Dunlops covering its 15 in. alloy wheels—original-size 16 inchers are now the order of the day at Lynx—SAL would have been quicker still; maybe even capable of cracking the five-second barrier to 60 mph. Certainly, away from the artificial sadism of Millbrook's mile straight, it felt every bit as rapid as a Testarossa or an Aston Zagato. It's ability to cover each of the 20 mph increments between 30 and 90 mph in top in little more than four seconds apiece

probably explains why.

On the road, the Lynx hauled in the horizon as if it was attached to a high-speed winch. Given half a chance, its bulbous snout devoured short straights with an almost savage disdain. Once moving, you could barely trust your senses: the solid shove in the back should have warned you, but until you matched your rhythm to the car's, bends arrived too quickly, brakes were worked too hard. They didn't seem to mind, remaining firm, powerful and seemingly unfadeable. Just as well.

For lovers of the twin-cam straight-six, the Lynx was a kind of Valhalla. It grumbled, it spat, it howled and it grunted. But above everything was a mechanical purity you couldn't find anywhere else, a euphony that contrasted starkly with the sharp, metallic edge of an Italian V12. There was an alluring gentility, too. Snick the stubby, machined-aluminium gear knob forward into first, ease out the meaty, but progressive, clutch and the Lynx trickled off at idle into the lethargy of the rush hour without a murmur of dissent.

Into second, then third: the shift was easy and fluid, the engine smooth and strong without the sense of frenzy that often accompanies latent fury. Capable of pushing the D-Type through the air at over 160 mph? Almost certainly, though SAL's particular gearing suggested a rev-limited top-end of around 150 mph. It was enough. The D-Types at Le Mans could brush 200 mph, but SAL was suffering from a worn limited-slip differential when I drove it, which invariably precipitated a worrying weave to the left when the throttle was eased. That said, grip was never found wanting, and the steering made up in feel for what it lacked in precision—and that wasn't much. The Lynx was beautifully neutral in fast sweeps and, in tighter bends, that legendary D-Type 'driftability' had been preserved, too. All this and a decent ride.

The Lynx D-Type was one of those rare cars that shook up your emotions and rode roughshod over rationality. It left you aching with desire. That much, at least, was the real thing.

Lotus Esprit Turbo

Ferrari, Lamborghini and Porsche might hog the 'exoticar' spotlight, but not to the exclusion of a small specialist car maker near Norwich: Lotus. In many ways, the Esprit Turbo has always been 'The Thinking Man's Countach', and it's never been hard to see why.

Well, just think about it: the original was a mid-engined wedge styled by an Italian master (in this case Giugiaro, the Countach was Bertone). Even the latest version is very low, very wide, very awkward to see out of and very fast. It has track-car reflexes and can generate more lateral grip than just about any other car in production. The one that comes closest is the low, wide, hard-to-see-out-of, very fast, Italian-styled, mid-engined wedge called the Countach. All right, make that extremely fast . . . and

four times the price of the Esprit. The comparison will always favour the British car.

Of course, the Lotus upsets the apple-cart: it is both overtly a senior-league exotic and a bargain. In Italy and Germany, no such synthesis has ever happened, nor is it ever likely to. The Esprit was born out of an essentially minimalist concept, and its simplicity and efficiency shine through. Like the Ferrari Dino, it does more with less.

Naturally, the plastic-bodied Esprit isn't perfect—its wheelbase is just a little stubby for ideal proportioning, the classically sharp-edged Giugiaro styling was softened and sanitized in-house for the 1987 model, it feels less 'crafted' than 'assembled' and, when all is said and done, it only has four cylinders, 2.2 litres and a turbocharger for muscles.

But then so has the modern Grand Prix car. And how many of them are powered by Lamborghini?

Lotus Esprit Turbo

Layout: four-cylinder, mid-mounted, rear drive
Top speed: 145 mph
0–60 mph: 5.4 sec
Economy: 18 mpg
Visual presence: 8
Aural presence: 4
Dynamic rating: 9
Charisma rating: 6
Sum-up: A Countach for a quarter of the price.

Speed kings

'The twin-turbo, 478 bhp F40 was the most expedient way of saying "yarboo sucks" to those arrogant Germans.'

'If there was a Daytona 'ere,' said the people's philosopher in the black blouson jacket, 'it would 'ave that well beat. No problem.'

'Maybe, maybe not,' I replied in a pre-combative trauma, 'but Ferrari don't make it any more, do they?' My friendly interrogator couldn't disagree.

'Hmmmm. . . . Pity. Well, must be goin'. Give it some. You know, shag the tarmac.' I didn't and I'm not sure I wanted to. The cocky Cockney flicked one of the Lamborghini's gumball P7s with an oil-stained trainer and shuffled off, hands in pockets, to insult the Porsche Turbo.

Standing alone again, I contemplated the immediate future. Which was the world's swiftest

Ferrari pledged to make only 200 GTOs, but Niki Lauda wanted one, so they made some more. Courtesy *Motor*/**Rowe**

production supercar, Porsche 911 Turbo, Aston Martin V8 Vantage, Lotus Esprit Turbo or Lamborghini Countach LP500 S? The next hour would tell.

The morning had the surreal, distant quality of a lucid dream. The stage and its props, to borrow a theatrical analogy, seemed familiar enough, but the plot was bizarre, the players outrageous and the audience improbable. Parked in a dense group in one corner of the paddock, four Lamborghini Countach LP 500s—one white, one black and two red—glistened expensively (to the tune of £236,000) in the watery sunshine. Such a sight would have been unusual in the exoticar Mecca of Modena. In a quiet backwater of rural Essex, people rubbed their eyes.

But then, this was no regular Saturday at North Weald Aerodrome. Three of the Lambos were merely doing what they were best at: posing. The fourth, one of the red ones, belonged to Barry Robinson. It

World's Fastest Supercar? Countach, Vantage, Esprit Turbo or 911 Turbo? Lamborghini had to give best to

...rsche on the day of reckoning. Courtesy *Motor*/Burn

was BR 33, the infamous 'blueprinted' 5-litre car he owned before the Quattrovalvole that starred in Chapter 1. BR 33 had already lifted a pile of national speed records at the Millbrook proving ground, driven by Barry himself, and turned in a set of acceleration figures at MIRA that made *Motor*'s then road test editor Jeremy Sinek's eyes water. It had come to North Weald to defend Modenese honour in the second staging of 'The World's Fastest Supercar' contest—an event won the previous year by this year's spectating black Countach.

The conspicuous presence of the Countach contingent was itself testimony to the owners' unflinching belief in its superiority and their enthusiasm for the snorting bull marque. It seemed that a large portion of the captive crowd, who had come to see an air display and stayed to witness the supercar showdown, were rooting for the Italian job, too. My task was to make sure the Lamborghini won. No one actually gave me a knowing wink, but I now reckon that everyone directly concerned with the preparation of BR 33 believed the car to be so good, so invincible, that all it required to win was for someone to sit in the driver's seat. And that was only to comply with the rules of the contest. I comforted myself with the thought that the short betting on the Lambo was at last partly due to my being in control of the steering wheel. The programme billed me as a 'fast start expert', after all.

What followed out on the runway, I'm told, had a certain savage beauty (smoking tyres, soaring revs, snatched shifts) tinged with sniggering embarrassment (I almost stalled the Countach on my second run). Within the space of half an hour, however, the burning issue had been settled. Porsche's 911 Turbo was quicker over the standing kilometre than the Countach. Not by much (23.98 seconds versus 24.31 seconds), but by enough to rule out the influence of driver technique.

Everyone could tell that the Porsche was exceptionally rapid just by looking at the way in which it devoured the kilometre (and subsequently I found out why ... what's sauce for the goose), but the result still came as something of a shock, not least to the Lamborghini camp who held me personally responsible for its victory. Naturally, I was disappointed not to be able to spray them all with champagne. Lotus pilot Roger Becker, however, was the man who most looked like he needed a drink after his Esprit Turbo seemed to be heading for a new world land-speed record on its very first run preparatory to expiring in a pall of white vapour. Draw your own conclusion. The people's philosopher looked disappointed, too. He was still kicking around the paddock as I packed away my overalls. There was no mistaking the 'told-you-so' twinkle in his eyes.

The interesting thing to me wasn't so much that the Porsche had pipped the Lambo, but that so many people regarded it as the most significant event since the resurrection. Who knows? A good Daytona might have edged them both over the kilometre and would certainly have thrashed them on top speed. It wouldn't have made the Countach and 911 lesser cars, or the Ferrari a greater one. Yet an obsession with big figures seems to be an essential element of the public's love affair with the supercar, none more so than *top speed*. All right, perhaps the Countach should be a little faster than it is, but it isn't the end of the world.

The stakes in this particular automotive game have risen considerably over the past few years. 'Off-the-peg' exotics like Ferrari's Testarossa (181 mph, sensational engine, tremendous road presence) and the Countach Quattrovalvole (over 170 mph, slightly less sensational engine, the ultimate road presence) were no push-overs, and both possessed that essential ingredient for credibility among those who can afford them: to cost as much as a decent house.

But by the mid-1980s, 'Testarossa' and 'Countach' were no longer the last words in four-wheeled extravagance. Aston Martin's Zagato had the Italian pair beaten on grounds of claimed speed and price alone, exceeding the Ferrari's maximum by a comfortable 6 mph and its price by a cool £25,000 in

1986. Unfortunately for the British car, a faster
Ferrari had been around for the best part of a year.
For a while, the limited-edition twin-turbo GTO
(190 mph, heart-stopping engine, unutterably
beautiful) had an unshakeable grasp on the 'ultimate
possession' laurels and proved so desirable, even at
£75,000 in the UK, that Ferrari were persuaded that
to make just 200 was a crime against filthy-rich
humanity and a few dozen more wouldn't harm
existing owners' investments. Niki Lauda was first
in the queue.

Perhaps he should have waited. Almost before the
ink had dried on his cheque, the GTO was
comprehensively upstaged by Porsche's Group 4
homologation special, the 959 (197 mph, high-tech
turbo power to all four wheels, other-world styling)
which, at £155,000, must have looked suicidally
expensive, even to those who wouldn't think twice

**Aston Zagato's styling grows on some observers.
Not this one. Courtesy _Motor_/Rowe**

Following pages **Porsche's hi-tech 959—a racing
car for the road. Courtesy _Motor_/Burn**

about spending £10,000 on a record player for the conservatory.

Unsurprisingly, Ferrari were not best pleased at this turn of events and, under a flimsy veil of secrecy, set about redressing the status-quo. It didn't take them long. From conception to realization spanned just 12 months, at the end of which the F40 was announced to a slack-jawed world. The F40 was so named to celebrate the fortieth anniversary of the Ferrari factory. To enhance its sense of historical perspective, Ferrari billed it as the logical production development of their experimental *Evoluzione*, itself a radical development of the 190 mph GTO. No one familiar with the way Ferrari do things was buying that story. Rather, the twin-turbo, 478 bhp F40 was the most expedient way of saying 'yarboo sucks' to those arrogant Germans. It cost £153,000 and would do 201.3 mph, so there. The real irony is that Ferrari briefed Pininfarina to make the F40 look like a Le Mans racer, yet Maranello have no intention of racing it. It's those big numbers again: they make cynics out of honourable men.

Two-hundred miles an hour is now the meaningful figure, the once 'magic ton' having long since become just another acceleration statistic. I harbour an awful suspicion that there are people for whom the alleged 4 mph difference in top speed between the Porsche 959 and Ferrari F40 is crucial. The terrible fascination is to be able to see a '2' in front of that pair of zeros. I can only think that it's the Chuck Yeager syndrome, the goal being to extend the envelope, to be the fastest, to wear a pair of Ray Ban Aviators.

An event portentously dubbed 'The Gathering of Eagles' did some serious envelope extending one bright and sunny day during the summer of 1987 in Ohio, USA. At a giant oval test track belonging to the

A better way to start the day . . . if this is what you see when you look out of your bedroom window every morning. Courtesy *Motor*/**Rowe**

Transportation Research Center, some of the fastest road cars in America assembled to slug it out. A similar exercise, staged mostly with European exoticars at VW/Audi's Ehra Lessien test facility, had seen a heavily-modified Porsche 911 Turbo do 211.5 mph and a 959 confirm the factory's 197 mph claim. Therefore, anything without a serious claim on the double-ton couldn't really be taken seriously at 'The Gathering'. Nevertheless, with the 959 not on sale in America, and the Ferrari F40 too new to make an appearance, it was left to the good ol' Ferrari Testarossa to represent standard European exoticar interests in the trial of speed. Indeed, it was the *only* standard supercar of the six, and one that was slightly below par at that, as it couldn't be coaxed above 172.9 mph. Embarrassingly for the Maranello camp, an AMG-modified Mercedes—the innocuous-looking 300 saloon powered by a 6-litre quad-cam V8, driving through a four-speed automatic box—made a better showing with an entirely respectable maximum of 181.4 mph. However, the inevitable tweaked lightweight 911 Turbo (a Ruf conversion with further work by Motorsport Design of Arizona) put in a convincing 202.5 mph. The figures become meaningless after a while, don't they?

For the Yanks there were a couple of Chevrolet Corvettes from Callaway Cars Inc, who build the twin-turbo version sold by Chevrolet, and a Camaro with a ridiculously swollen power bulge on its bonnet. Nothing too much for the super-hi-tech 959 driver to worry about, there. Or so you might have thought. That Camaro, it had an 8.9-litre V8 developing 690 bhp. Then there was the 'nearly standard' Corvette Twin Turbo with around 400 bhp and the 'nearly NASCAR' version with 712 bhp. Now perhaps you can appreciate why it's pointless losing sleep over the fact that your £170,000 motor car will only do 197 mph. Against these brutes, it's not even in the same race. This American trio was to supercardom what a double Big Mac with large fries and triple-thick shake are to nouvelle cuisine—you simply can't beat calories. Even the lesser of the two

Above **Gone in 60 seconds, about what it took the Callaway Corvette to reach its staggering top speed of 224 mph. Courtesy** *Fast Lane*

Left **The most remarkable supercar there has ever been, Porsche's 197 mph 959. Courtesy** *Motor*/**Burn**

Corvettes did 191.7 mph, the faster an astonishing 224.4 mph, or faster than a contemporary Grand Prix car—all on 5.8 litres, two turbos and vast quantities of petrol. The 9-litre Camaro? A modest 216 mph.

Me? I'd take the AMG Merc, pull into the slow lane and turn up the stereo if I saw a 959 in the mirror, its driver refusing to move over for an F40 and Callaway Corvette locked in an eyeball stare at 200 mph. I like a car that knows its limitations.

The Porsche 959 is simply the greatest and most able supercar to date. It costs as much as a decent house but, for that, you get a car that pulls no punches: it's as good as current technology can make it, and that's a great deal better than anything else, including Ferrari's F40 (200 mph top speed notwithstanding).

That it looks like a sat-on 911 is no coincidence. The size, lightness and engine of the 911 were important starting points. The compromises inherent in that car's design have been exorcized by sheer weight of engineering, but the compact, quirky cabin, awkward controls and '911-ness' largely remain, as does an air-cooled flat-six engine installed in what would be most cars' boot. Yes, you can trace the 959's basic design principles back to the VW Beetle!

Computer-controlled four-wheel drive, a six-speed gearbox, a Kevlar and aluminium body, two turbochargers and 450 bhp are what the 959 are all about. The unrivalled combination of power and traction make it the only production car made that can accelerate from a standstill to 60 mph in under four seconds. But that's just a party trick. What this Porsche is really good at is distorting long-held frames of reference and notions of what is possible on four wheels. It actually fulfils what must be many a schoolboy's fantasy: to have racing-car performance on ordinary roads—not just in straight-line

speed, but cornering and braking, too. To have so great a margin of superiority over other road users is the drug—the feeling of control and safety it brings, especially since the Porsche's remarkable talents are so accessible.

It's a new kind of motoring, and the 959 is a new kind of car. It can't quite manage 200 mph, by the way.

Porsche 959

Layout: flat-six, rear-mounted, four-wheel drive
Top speed: 197 mph
0–60 mph: 3.9 sec
Economy: 15 mpg
Visual presence: 8
Aural presence: 8
Dynamic rating: 10
Charisma rating: 7
Sum-up: Together with the Ferrari F40, the only car to distance itself from the supercar herd. The greatest supercar there has ever been, despite some turbo lag. The scores for the F40, incidentally, would have been 9, 7, 9 and 7.

Masters of disguise

'The M5 was a cold-blooded killer dressed as a Harley Street consultant.'

The Mike Spence Uno and the AMG 560E Hammer prove, beyond all doubt, that some of the deadliest movers are studies in plainness, and deliberately deceptive. The generic term is 'Q-car', and the effect of its deceit is often devastating. In essence, the Q-car is a supercar in disguise, yet the very fact that it eschews the single-minded, no-compromise styling and engineering conventions of the breed sets it apart.

Take the original BMW M5—the archetypal Q-car. The brilliance of its 24-valve engine was taken for granted. But did 286 bhp make the M5 a supercar in the conventional sense? Consider the facts.

Acceleration: breathtaking. Ground-covering potential: unmatched in the four-seater ranks. Handl-

M6 combined pace and elegance to great effect. Courtesy *Fast Lane*

ing: as consistent as it was forgiving. Seldom had so much raw potency and dynamic ability been wrapped-up in such a sober, conservatively-cut package. The M5 was studiously classy without being fastidiously flashy, a cold-blooded killer dressed as a Harley Street consultant.

Everything was calculated for maximum efficiency and precision, nothing for effect. No traces of extrovert flamboyance had been allowed to penetrate the fortress of Bavarian urbanity. Even the subtle spoilers and fine-latticed wheels of the svelte M6 coupe, which had the same engine, had no place on the M5 as supplied by the factory. The disguise was perfect and impregnable.

BMW's attention to detail rendered the M5 more civilized than any car of comparable performance. To drive it was to appreciate the qualities that made the 5-series such a competent executive saloon: the superb driving position, the flawless ergonomics,

M Power: says it all. Courtesy *Motor*/Burn

the clarity of the instruments, the tactile precision of the switches. But it was also to know the arch-conservatism that permeated BMW's oldest model range. The shape, never pretty, seemed too staid and upright, its packaging well behind a Ford Granada's, its prestige dulled by familiarity. Both to behold and to sit in, the M5 lacked the tacky-palm inspiration of a sleeker machine with a hot Latin bloodline. There was no sense of occasion in unlocking the door and slipping easily behind the large wheel, no tingling edge of fear that the power might overwhelm, no apprehension about seeing out or mastering a difficult gear-change, no hint of exotic sophistication as the 24-valve straight-six fired up and settled to a slightly lumpy, but otherwise unremarkable, tickover. All to the good as far as I was concerned.

Such was the initial understatement that it made the M5 seem dull when it was, in fact, highly

charged. In traffic, the big engine was a model of docility, a gentle and untemperamental force. But watch the revs soar when you floor the throttle, listen to the engine note change from soft to hard, and then a hollow cry. When the M5 charged, the body language was right, and nothing from Modena or Maranello could scratch out the high-performance message with more eloquence.

Yet *real* excitement tends to be inferior. BMW's method, which was to assemble a collection of virtues and polish out any natural imperfections, painted a diamond-hard lacquer between the driver and the deeper levels of the M5's soul. The secret of Italy's best supercars—even those which are badly finished, ergonomically flawed and hard to see out of—is their 'wholeness', the harmony between form and speed, a coherence of spirit and steel. The M5 was too busy being a BMW to offer its driver these root-level rewards, too detached for intimacy.

BMW M635 CSi was the first of the 'cooking' models to use the M1's mighty 286 bhp, 24-valve straight-six. Courtesy *Motor*/**Burn**

The M5's forte was playing two disparate roles with equal slickness, concealing a granite fist in a velvet glove. But such breadth of purpose rendered the M5 somewhat cold and clinical. It tamed the fury of a magnificent engine, controlling it to the point where every last ounce of power was as ordered as the digits on a compact disc. Extracting all the performance was as easy as taking sweets from a child. You marvelled at the sheer generosity of it all but, at the same time, felt cheated.

The M5's strengths were essentially no different to those of its spiritual forebear, the Mercedes 450 SEL 6.9—the saloon which ruled the autobahns in the late 1970s: huge straight-line speed, deliberate aesthetic understatement, and unwavering all-round competence. Like the Merc, only discreet badges revealed the true scope of its performance and, in so doing, reinforced the peculiarly Teutonic ethos that serious performance motoring only begins when the throttles are opened wide.

They wouldn't open any wider one memorable day in Germany behind the wheel of a Mercedes 560 SEC. The blazing headlights that had been closing in for the past ten minutes were suddenly holding station 20 metres behind. Almost embarrassingly, a small, persistently winking amber eye, barely visible in the tumbling spray kicked up by our Mercedes' fat P6 tyres, signalled that they wanted to slip past. I felt threatened. . . .

How could my progress be bettered? I was driving hard along one of the increasingly rare stretches of unrestricted autobahn feeding Stuttgart from the north, in what many would rate as the German motor city's finest statement of power and prestige. The weather was filthy, a dizzying barrack-drill of snow, sleet and swirling rain under an army-blanket sky. The tauntingly warm breezes posing as spring in Stuttgart just 24 hours earlier had given way to the Christmas-card scenes of Bremen, from where we had come. Yet we could name no car more equal to

Mercedes' coupé flagship, the 560 SEC. Iron fist, velvet glove. Courtesy *Motor*/Rowe

the conditions than the one in which we were travelling, unchallenged by anything on two wheels or four in nearly 700 kilometres of who-dares-wins autobahn blasting.

And blast we did in the 560 SEC. If so commanded, Mercedes' V8-engined supercoupé would, we discovered, make any hot-shot BMW 735i saloon shrink like an Alka Seltzer in a bowl of acid. The familiar, pouting Bavarian nose might thrust at the Mercedes' neat rump with predatory intent, but its rear-view-mirror image would collapse to sub-Dinky-toy proportions within seconds of the appropriate pedal having been applied to the metal (or durable thick-pile carpet in this case). We were too fast for all but the 24-valve Motorsport BMWs and most non-turbocharged Porsches. But how fast was that?

The mighty 5.6-litre V8 powerhouse was calculated to elevate the sleek Swabian coupé to the elite ranks of the $150+$ mph club. Based on the existing 5-litre unit, the new engine's longer stroke gave it a swept volume of 5547 cc and, in high-compression (10.0:1), free-breathing tune, it developed 300 bhp at 5000 rpm, an increase of no less than 30 per cent on the 500's 231 bhp and on arm-wrestling terms with a V12 Jaguar's 299 bhp. Maximum torque was an even more impressive 336 lb ft at 3750 rpm, sufficient for Mercedes' excellent four-speed automatic transmission to start off in second unless the accelerator was floored.

The 560 was certainly the car to have in bustling rush-hour Bremen. The tyre-screeching alacrity of its step-off from rest was impressive, even against a background of high expectations, and made us almost invincible in any traffic-light Grand Prix or scrap for an opening gap. I always thought the XJ-S was good in this respect, but the Mercedes felt better with a faster, more solid response to the throttle.

It was confirmed within half an hour on the autobahn: 0–30 mph in 2.5 seconds—exceptional for an automatic and bettered, in our experience, only by the similarly-powerful, but almost absurdly torquey, Bentley Mulsanne Turbo (2.2 seconds). In fact, comparisons with the leviathan Brit were instructive. At 60 mph, the Bentley was still ahead (6.7 seconds against 7.1 seconds), but with the 560 gaining ground rapidly and inexorably. By 100 mph, the charging Teuton had closed down the Mulsanne with a time of 16.6 seconds (18.9 seconds) and, from there on, it was the Mercedes all the way. The real measure of the 560's towering performance was its 0–120 mph time of just 24.0 seconds, putting it on level terms with the Porsche 928S (23.7 seconds) and decisively ahead of Jaguar's XJ-S (26.6 seconds), not to mention the old 500 SEC (36.6 seconds).

But as we merged into the strands of traffic on the outskirts of town, the other side of the SEC's character—registered only subliminally on the way out in the wake of fierce anticipation over the performance figures—filtered back, and with it disappointment. Although a quiet car on the surface (*Motor*'s noise meter doesn't lie), it wasn't a refined one by the standards of its class: there was too much vibration—through the toeboard, through the accelerator pedal, through the gear selector. This was all the more regrettable in the light of the efforts Mercedes had exerted to eliminate the road roar that so often flawed their products. With the SEC, they very nearly succeeded. Coarse-surface tarmac still excited a muted thrumming from the broad-shouldered tyres but, for much of the time, the suspension worked quietly and wind noise was extremely well suppressed, even at high, three-figure cruising speeds.

There simply wasn't the space to extract the little extra straight-line speed on tap before the weather closed in again and, drive as fast as I dare, the blazing headlights on our tail just wouldn't go away. There was nothing left but to pull over and let them pass. Predictably, it wasn't just one car but two in fast convoy. A quick mental calculation as they streaked by, engines wailing exultantly, put their combined value at £300,000. There was little point in giving chase, since both were capable of nearly 200 mph. Not today, though. A few kilometres down the autobahn, the white Porsche 959s peeled off for Zuffenhausen and home.

It was a Monday, three years later, in downtown Budapest, 14 kilometres to the south west at Ferihegy airport, when BA-702 crabbed drunkenly through dirty puddles of low cloud, heaved queasily over stormy thermals and gave everyone on board a generally bad time. It landed with a thump and then landed again.

This was an ordinary 737 with no ordinary cargo. It bore a select group of westerners who tumbled down the gangway and were whisked discreetly away to a VIP lounge on the top floor of the lone terminal building. As they entered the lounge— most sporting dark glasses despite the gloomy lighting—video cameras from Hungarian television whirred into action and zoomed in on faintly worried faces. They zoomed out again when the director realized that what he had in his viewfinder were not the British Airways executives he had on his briefing card. They'd slipped in minutes earlier and were already quaffing champagne to celebrate BA's twentieth year of flying to Hungary. The imposters hogging air time were media men themselves and would have had a good story to tell had they been asked. The one about the 14 British motoring writers who flew all the way to the Eastern Bloc to drive £1,000,000-worth of Rolls Royce and Bentley motor cars.

Contrary to any reasonable assumption of what a handful of western motoring journalists might be up to behind the Iron Curtain, the main purpose was to assess, on a wholesale level, possibly the most outrageous Q-car of all, the £80,000 Bentley Mulsanne Turbo R—not, as might be anticipated, to gauge the reaction of locals to perhaps the most awesome expression of capitalist decadence ever assembled in a communist country, but to quantify the dynamic and cosmetic improvements of the 1987 model on a racing track. Not even Frederick Forsyth

Two tons of turbocharged muscle; Bentley's outrageous Mulsanne Turbo R. Courtesy *Fast Lane*

would buy this as a plot, but do this job for long enough and you realize that anything is possible.

Within 20 minutes we'd reached our destination: the Hungaroring, the only Grand Prix circuit in the Eastern Bloc, which was built in just 18 months at a cost of £5,300,000. All 16 Bentleys would be out on the track at the same time: 32 tons of turbocharged metal and leather, 64 screaming Avon Turbospeed tyres, £1,280,000 looking for an accident.

The heavily-padded leather throne I was sitting on had been reshaped to provide more lateral support. Moreover, its powered eight-way adjustment now incorporated a memory function for the four preferred seat positions. Unfortunately, none of these offered the possibility of sitting in a café in the centre of Budapest. The adjusters worked well, moving silkily to the touch of the Mercedes-like 'seat graphic' control. As other members of the Rolls-Royce party fired up and woofled out, I could think of no good reason not to follow them. Five laps later, brakes smoking and tyres rooted, I could think of several.

According to RR's information pack, the Hungaroring is 4014 metres long with 20 bends—12 right, eight left. The shortest curve is 20 metres, the longest 400 metres. The main straight is 700 metres long and good for 200 mph if you're Nigel Mansell behind the wheel of a Williams. Behind the wheel of a Mulsanne Turbo, the Hungaroring was the longest understeering slide in the world. The tyres started squealing the moment you braked for the first downhill, off-camber right-hander at the end of the straight and didn't stop until you entered it again after a constant-radius loop so long it's a wonder the tyres hadn't decided to call it a day, rolled off their rims and applied for exit visas.

It was a phenomenon that two tons of Mulsanne Turbo would even look at the Hungaroring, and a mercy that it sacrificed its tyres and brake pads before your author. Safe and forgiving it may have been, enjoyable and entertaining it was not. Quite what RR were expecting to prove by exposing a car not previously noted for its handling prowess to the twistiest Grand Prix circuit in the world I don't know, but they must have been relieved when it was over.

The Hungaroring proved exactly why road cars, especially big, heavy and fast ones, can be comprehensively wrong-footed by the artificiality of a racing circuit. The Bentley *felt* underpowered, undertyred and underbraked when, in more realistic conditions, you would expect it to be none of these things. The real pity was that the additional time with the Turbo R was confined to a quick blast down a stretch of two-lane motorway adjacent to the circuit. For this purpose, RR had come to an arrangement with the Hungarian authorities to waive the prevailing 100 kph limit. Some members of the Rolls-Royce party needed no persuading to wind the Turbo R's speedo needle off the end of its 150 mph scale—a speed most locals driving their Skodas, Ladas and Trabants had only witnessed watching 737s taking off from Ferihegy airport. For my part, it was enough to note that the big Bentley could procure effortless urge up to 120 mph, at which speed it still generated about 30 per cent more wind noise than a Jaguar XJ6.

Back in the executive coach, the traditional Hungarian apricot brandy was broken out for the 15 kilometre journey back to the Budapest Hilton. The hazards of the afternoon were quickly forgotten as Esther, our pretty young guide, expounded the relevant facts about Budapest and Hungary. In the light of the luxury to which all of us had so quickly become accustomed, it came as something of a shock to learn that the average Hungarian wage was 5000 Ft, or £66 a month. This, it transpired, was every bit as bad as it sounds since, in automotive matters at least, the cost of living is considerably worse than we're used to in the UK. A gallon of petrol in Hungary, for instance, costs £1.20, and a basically-equipped Lada, £2000, or the equivalent of two years' salary. It took only a couple of seconds with a calculator to work out that the average Hungarian would have to work for 100 years and devote his entire remuneration to the purpose of buying a car to afford a Mulsanne Turbo. Unless he was a personal friend of the local police chief, it's not an enterprise I would readily have recommended.

The outskirts of Budapest were considerably more attractive than anything I'd seen so far, and the city itself fully deserved the description of magnificent. Our coach jostled for position with trams, on which it cost the equivalent of only a few pence to travel down avenues lined with fashionably-dressed shoppers who might easily have emerged from hotels equipped with their own natural thermal spas operating at a temperature between 28 and 30 degrees Celsius. The city possessed a rare sense of scale and grandeur as well as an architectural coherence in which the grime accumulated over decades of two-stroke emissions from Wartburgs and Trabants had dressed the neo-Gothic facades with a layer of soot that seemed entirely in keeping with the *gravitas* of the city.

We had a good time, but you'd never have guessed it.

Bentley Turbo R was too big and bulky for the tight and twisty Hungaroring. Tyres smoked while the author dreamed of a café in downtown Budapest

BMW M5

To a greater extent than the dashingly-styled current version, the original M5 seemed far too prim and proper to assume the taxing, tough role of Porsche-slayer. With its ageing, staid and boxy four-door body, its studied plainness and almost obsessive absence of 'go-faster' addenda—save for those fine-lattice alloy wheels and the Motorsport badges—you'd have thought this most deceptive of all BMWs would have had trouble competing effectively with its executive-class peers, never mind the world's most accomplished road burners.

This was the natural reaction to a visually boring car, but what it failed to recognize was crucial: the M5 was a living lie, the consummate Q-car, a world-class sprinter in a wheelchair. For beneath that oh-so-reserved exterior lay the 3.5-litre, twin-cam, 24-valve, 286 bhp straight-six that, in its original (and less powerful) form, powered perhaps the greatest road-going BMW of all: the M1.

The figures were eloquent testimony to the M5's true potential—0–60 mph in 5.9 seconds, 0–100 mph in 15.8 seconds, a top speed of 155 mph.

It was all smothered by false modesty. Yet BMW's traditional attention to detail rendered the M5 more civilized than *any* car of comparable performance. To drive it was to appreciate the qualities that made the 5-Series models such competent executive saloons: the perfect driving position, the superb ergonomics, the clarity of the instruments, the tactile precision of the switchgear. It was a magnificent disguise.

In the end, though, that M5 lacked a certain something. That even temperament and smooth understatement had removed the natural imperfections. The M5 was, perhaps, too busy being a BMW to give its driver these root-level rewards. However, the alternative it offered was no less valid for that.

BMW M5

Layout: straight-six, front-mounted, rear drive
Top speed: 151 mph
0–60 mph: 5.9 sec
Economy: 18 mpg
Visual presence: 3
Aural presence: 7
Dynamic rating: 8
Charisma rating: 6
Sum-up: Probably the best Q-car in the world.

I've seen the future and it's a Toyota

'The cutting edge of technology is moving forward with greater haste than at any time in the car's history.'

Media analysts have never successfully established whether *Knight Rider*, the television fantasy for kids, irrevocably manipulated the minds of Japan's under-12s. In *Knight Rider*, the good guy, Michael Knight, was constantly upstaged by his computerized automotive side-kick 'Kitt'—a deceptive black Pontiac which talked, drove itself, flew through the air and generally seemed more capable of wasting Porsche-driving bad guys than the hapless and gangling Knight. The decision-making executives at Toyota must have been *Knight Rider* junkies. There seems no other plausible explanation for the existence of the Toyota Soarer, a high-tech haemorrhage disguised by the unremarkable presence of an ostensibly normal and unassuming

No, not a scene from the sci-fi thriller *Blade Runner*, but the Toyota Soarer on a wet night in Tokyo. A sweet and sour taste of the future

executive coupé with svelte styling and an impressively powerful turbocharged engine.

It didn't talk (frankly, a surprise) and it didn't drive itself (a mere detail). Otherwise, the Soarer was as close to the TV fantasy car as made no difference. This side of a film set, there has never been a car like the Soarer and, this side of the Atlantic ocean, it's unlikely that there ever will be. By and large, the Japanese kept the world's most technically sophisticated car to themselves and a few sympathetic markets. Belgium, for instance. That's where *Motor*'s Japanese correspondent, Kevin Radley, stopped off *en route* to London from Tokyo a few years back to swap a 747 for the altogether more complex Soarer 3.0 GT Limited, positively the last word in Toyota's flagship range and an intriguing vision of tomorrow through the eyes of today's technologists.

That the Soarer 3.0 GT Limited (the 'Limited' referred to its production run, not its commercial

status) wasn't actually blessed with the power of flight, as its name suggests, shouldn't be too disheartening. A Soarer is a glider, its elegance of style reflecting a beautiful simplicity of function. The Toyota Soarer floated on 'air suspension', a newly-developed double-wishbone arrangement at all four wheels, featuring an electronically-controlled pneumatic springing system with three stages of spring-rate adjustment and ride height, as well as variable damping—all of which was automatically administered according to road and driving conditions, unless the driver thought he knew better and overrode the system.

The rest of the chassis maintained the high standard of compound-nouns. Steering was by rack and pinion, but with electronically-modulated, speed-sensitive power-assistance. Braking was by ventilated discs all round with anti-lock as standard. The Soarer was a heavy car propelled by 227 bhp: it

Technology for the sake of it, or a genuine glimpse of tomorrow? The Toyota Soarer did everything but drive itself. Courtesy *Motor*/**Rowe**

Toyota's outstanding Celica GT-Four; more raw ability than any 'exotic' of ten years ago. Courtesy *Motor*/**Valente**

took some stopping. The power was generated by a turbocharged and intercooled version of the Supra's 3-litre, twin-cam straight-six with four directly-actuated valves per cylinder, fully-mapped electronic ignition and a fuel-injection system that used an optical airflow meter. It drove to the rear wheels via Toyota's three-mode (switchable overdrive, 'economy', 'sport'), electronically-controlled, four-speed automatic, the only transmission offered with the 3-litre engine.

All this hi-tech hardware was clothed by a surprisingly understated two-door coupé bodywork. The fine-lattice wheels (wearing useful 215/60 Pirelli P6s) looked fancy, and the rear light clusters were too fussy, but the shape itself was rather graceful and rendered 'clean' by its flush glass. Just how clean Toyota didn't say, but the claimed 140 mph top speed suggests a Cd of around 0.35.

As with *Knight Rider*'s smart-arse 'Kitt', though,

the plain exterior served only to deceive. You had to climb inside to discover the real Soarer. At first, everything looked normal, plush, tasteful. But when you turned the ignition key to the first position, two things happened. First, the steering wheel—adjustable for rake, but not reach—zipped down a couple of inches on amazingly fast electric motors to assume the position it was last left in. Remove the ignition key and it zipped back up to the top of its travel to aid egress. Second, the inky-black binnacle behind the steering wheel where the instruments should have been winked into computerized

Status update on Soarer's built-in TV. If you couldn't read Japanese, you could always switch over to *EastEnders*. **Courtesy** *Motor*/**Rowe**

vibrance and introduced itself by doing everything it was capable of at the same time. Solid-state electronic instrument displays have slipped out of fashion for the time being, and probably for good, but that only serves to make the Soarer's all the more startling. It glowed with a limpid green electro-luminescence, the digits and bar graphs appearing to hang in free space—an illusion created by reflecting them on a half mirror.

The centre console was more fascinating still. It housed a touch-sensitive panel which glowed green like the instruments and controlled the stereo system and air conditioning, when they weren't controlling themselves. Then there was the television. No humourless CRT, this, but a decent 6 in. colour monitor that searched for TV stations like a good radio locks on to successive signals up the tuning scale. There was even a remote control for anyone prepared to squeeze into the cramped back seats to watch *EastEnders*. Possibly more entertaining than Dirty Den, however, were the on-screen status reports for economy, maintenance schedules and the operation of the computer-controlled suspension as springs, dampers and ride height were adjusted to cope with the on-going road conditions. The latter was a full-colour animation of the Soarer travelling west with large arrows indicating whether you were going up or down at any given moment in time.

Just as you were coming to terms with all this, though, you discovered that the cassette player did more than simply play music. It doubled as a data player for cassette-borne maps and an illustrated explanation of the car's on-board electronic systems. The map facility shouldn't be confused with the laser-digital navigation systems now being developed to guide you through the rush hour by the most efficient route—such technology was beyond the reach even of the Soarer. As for the explanation, it was all in Japanese.

No doubt, it mentioned the electronic winkers that signalled engagement with a friendly 'peep' rather than a mechanical click. And the LCD-modulated day-night mirror. Not forgetting the row of seven buttons mounted on the steering wheel boss which duplicated the functions of the touch-sensitive audio/air-conditioning control panel.

You were mentally exhausted even before you started to drive. Fortunately, the Soarer was instantly soothing. The soft and deceptive, well-shaped leather seats were superbly comfortable, the driving-position ergonomics hard to fault. All-round visibility was excellent, too, thanks to the deep glazing and slim pillars.

Nor did the Soarer's performance disappoint. It might have weighed the best part of 1½ tons, but it was fast: not quite Porsche 928 league, but tantalizingly close and accelerative enough to blow off any indigenous Japanese competition. The 24-valve straight-six was beautifully smooth—much smoother than the normally-aspirated Supra's—and with minimal lag and a responsive four-speed auto, not obviously turbocharged. The power flowed with a surge very reminiscent of a Jaguar XJ-S. That said, kickdown could sometimes be a little fierce, irrespective of the 'economy'/'sport' mode setting.

The computer-controlled air suspension had two

Mid-four ergonomics are definitely of this decade. Courtesy *Motor*/Radley

Nissan mid-four. The shape of things to come from Japan? Courtesy *Motor*/**Radley**

separate chambers in each spring unit, connected by small and large orifices, and provided a broad range of spring rates, as well as height and attitude control. The benefits of such a system were more apparent in the ride quality than they were in handling. The former was uniformly supple and well controlled— subjectively a cross between a Lotus Excel and a Citroën CX—the latter prone to strong understeer and body roll in tight bends, though never upset by bumps, no matter how severe. Grip was good, but probably no better than a Supra's.

In the final analysis, it was the Supra that provided the most telling testimony to the Soarer's role in life. Equipped with the Soarer's suspension and engine, the Supra would have been, without question, the finest Japanese car of the 1980s: lean, good looking tremendously fast—virtually a half-price 928. The Soarer, good as it was, failed to make the grade. Its designers' obsession with Hollywood gimmicks not only made it heavy, but heavy-going. Some of the technology it embodied was ingenious, but much of it was indulgent, ostentatious and vulgar.

Toyota had the technology, all right, but they didn't know what to do with it. Or at least it seemed that way at the time. Since the Soarer, the Japanese have welcomed four-wheel steering with open arms, pushed on with the development of true, computer-controlled active suspension, and advanced the concept of 'variable technology'—the sort of micro-processor-based engineering which will eventually lead to engines with adjustable compression ratios and cylinder capacities.

The cutting edge of technology is moving forward

'Technology and imagination', but will show cars like the Mitsubishi X25 ever see the light of day? Courtesy *Motor*/**Radley**

with greater haste than at any time during the car's history. So fast, in fact, that the first-generation four-wheel steering systems from Honda and Mazda will soon seem as crude as the 78 rpm record is to the compact disc. It's but a short step from four-wheel drive, four-wheel steering, active suspension, anti-lock brakes and anti-slip differentials—all of which are today's technology—to the fully 'intelligent' chassis, which is tomorrow's. The 'intelligent' chassis will literally out-think the road, each wheel steering and following surface contours inde-pendently of the others to optimize suspension geometry and minimize the influence of that most unpredictable of all variables: the driver. Computers and sensors will assume the vital roles.

Beyond that, and the Japanese are already working on it, is the driverless car. The germ of *Knight Rider* and countless science-fiction scenarios is already earmarked for a future time in this dimension. By then, road accidents will be history and, let's face it, so will the car as an object of desire and source of satisfaction.

Until then, we can count on new technology to continue the escalation of baseline standards. The evolution of the ordinary car will eventually see it eclipse traditional supercar abilities on its way to becoming a machine that works better without a driver at all. Then we'll all try to remember what it was like to sit in a Ford Sierra Cosworth or an Aston Zagato. Or anything … with a steering wheel, a brake pedal and, most important of all, an accelerator.

Aston Vantage Zagato

Although it looks like a forgotten Lancia Beta coupé styling study, the Zagato is, in fact, a brilliant anachronism. It completely and engagingly captures the spirit of the great, front-engined Grand Tourers of the 1960s and 1970s. Since Aston Martin, together with Ferrari, Maserati and a few other now defunct companies, were responsible for building the great,

front-engined Grand Tourers of the 1960s and 1970s, this is not altogether surprising.

Given Aston's desire to make a supercar to take on the very best from Italy and Germany, and given the raw material they had to work with, I'd have said they had a couple of options: either to embark on a cost-no-object, mid-engined, multi-turboed fantasy

along the hideously ugly lines of the ill-fated Bulldog, or to settle for a mild reworking of the existing V8 Vantage that merely looked radical. Sensibly, they plumped for the latter, tuning the Vantage's fabulous 5.3-litre quad-cam V8 to give 432 bhp, lightening its payload and employing the incomparable brothers Zagato to clothe a revised and shortened chassis with a distinctive two-door body. It's hard to believe that the men from Newport Pagnell asked for a Beta-lookalike with a power bulge in the bonnet and two 'bubbles' in the roof (Zagato's trademark) but, in essence, that's what they got.

No Beta ever went like the Aston Zagato, though. We're talking seriously fast: a top speed in excess of 175 mph and 0–60 mph in under five seconds. We're also talking nostalgia and charisma by the bulk-container load. The Zagato howls as only a car powered by a deep-chested, high-compression, quad-cam V8 can howl, and handles as only a car with a front-mounted engine delivering its enormous power to the rear wheels via a manual five-speed gearbox can handle.

Adult entertainment.

Aston Vantage Zagato

Layout: V8, front-mounted, rear drive
Top speed: 175 mph
0–60 mph: 4.9 sec
Economy: 12–15 mpg
Visual presence: 5
Aural presence: 10
Dynamic rating: 8
Charisma rating: 9
Sum-up: Last of the great British GTs. Fearsomely fast, but forgiving. Spine-tingling engine.